D1322695

Revise for PE GCSE for OCR

Frank Galligan, Eric Singleton, David White

L B W
WITHDRAWN
(BOOK-SALE)

501 403 075

Heinemann Educational Publishers
Halley Court, Jordan Hill, Oxford OX2 8EJ
Part of Harcourt Education

Heinemann is the registered trademark of
Harcourt Education Limited

Text © Frank Galligan, Eric Singleton, David White 2002

07
10 9 8 7

All rights reserved.

Apart from any fair dealing for the purposes of research or private study, or
criticism or review as permitted under the terms of the UK Copyright,
Designs and Patents Act, 1988, this publication may not be reproduced,
stored or transmitted, in any form or by any means, without the prior
permission in writing of the publishers, or in the case of reprographic
reproduction only in accordance with the terms of the licences issued by the
Copyright Licensing Agency in the UK, or in accordance with the terms of
licences issued by the appropriate Reproduction Rights Organization outside
the UK. Enquiries concerning reproduction outside the terms stated here
should be sent to the publishers at the address printed on this page.

British Library Cataloguing in Publication Data

A catalogue record for this book is available from the British Library

ISBN: 978 0 435100 43 8

Typeset by Techtype, Abingdon
Printed and bound in the UK by Scotprint

Acknowledgements

The publishers have made every effort to contact copyright holders. However,
if any material has been incorrectly acknowledged, the publishers would be
pleased to correct this at the earliest opportunity.

Tel: 01865 888058 www.heinemann.co.uk

LONDON BOROUGH OF WANDSWORTH	
501403075	
Askews	12-Jun-2008
796.07 GALL	£7.50
	WWX0003224/0001

Contents

How to use this book

This book has been specially produced for use in conjunction with *PE GCSE for OCR* and is laid out in such a way that topic headings and other sub-headings correspond to those used in that text. This should help you to feel that you are on 'familiar ground' – dealing with topics and terminology with which you have become accustomed.

The text highlights important areas of knowledge under a series of *Key Points* and the content of each area of study is graphically represented in each section to assist you in developing an overview. There are a small number of questions at the end of each section designed to test your knowledge and understanding of the material as well as *Key Words* that indicate specific points or meanings that you need to learn about.

Particular issues are highlighted in a number of *Focus Points*, which occur throughout the text and finally, each section contains a small number of *Exam Tips* written by the Chief Examiner. These suggest the kind of information/areas of study that you should be familiar with in order to be able to answer questions relevant to the topics in that section.

Clearly, however well-intentioned this book may be, it can only act as a guide and should not be regarded as a substitute for hard work and well-organised study and revision. In essence, revision should be ongoing. There is little point in studying a topic to return to it only when the examination is upon you. You should be continually refreshing and reviewing work done throughout the course so that your final revision period is founded upon sound knowledge rather than vague memories of work covered many months previously. The approach to revision outlined below should be of some assistance in helping you develop a consistent approach to your studies.

Revision strategy

The written examination at the end of your Physical Education GCSE course is important because it carries forty per cent of the overall marks available. In order to do well and achieve the grade you are hoping for, you will therefore need to perform well in this examination. This is only likely to be achieved if you plan carefully how you are going to prepare yourself for this important event.

Planning your revision should not be an *ad hoc* arrangement. It should be carefully thought out and planned at an early stage in your studies. If you do this and stick to your plan you will undoubtedly achieve greater success. So how do you plan a revision strategy?

In the first instance you should understand the theoretical content of the course you are following and how to apply different concepts to practical situations. During your course you will learn these concepts and be given opportunities to apply them in practical activity situations. You will also learn certain facts that you will need to remember. This *Revise for PE GCSE for OCR* text will provide you with a basis from which these concepts can be learned and remembered. One way that has been shown to be successful is to try to revise systematically as you go through the course – rather than in a panic right at the end. In this way you will study a 'chunk' or a topic of the course in your normal lessons and when this has been completed you will turn to the corresponding section in this text and read through it carefully, learning the section as well as you can. If you do not understand it first time, go through it again until you do. You should find that the concise way that the book has been set out should help you to remember all the important aspects of each topic.

You will then progress in your lessons to another aspect of the course. When this has been completed you should first re-read the previous topic before revising the current one. By doing this you will reinforce your knowledge of the previous topic before moving on. The matrix that follows might help you to see how the overlapping of revision sessions helps you to concentrate on specific topics in order to learn them thoroughly.

Topics to be learned	Topic 1	Topic 2	Topic 3	Topic 4
Revision	Revise Topic 1	Revise Topic 1 and Topic 2	Revise Topic 2 and Topic 3	Revise Topic 3 and Topic 4

By revising progressively in this way, you will be prepared for any tests or end of topic examinations that your teachers may present you with as part of your ongoing coursework.

Use the questions that occur after each topic in this book. Get a friend or a parent to test your knowledge by asking you the questions. If you are unsure then refer either to the student textbook, to this book, or where you are still unsure, to your teacher.

In the run up to the examination you will need to turn to the specimen examination papers at the end of this text. You can test yourself with either or both of the question papers but avoid reading the mark schemes that is given with both papers until you have completed them. Give yourself 2 hours to complete the specimen Physical Education (1970) Question Paper and 1 hour for the Physical Education: Games (Short Course)(1070) Question Paper. You will need to write on separate lined paper and be guided by the *Examination Tips* that can be found in the box to the right of the questions. When you have completed the test and read through your answers, you can then mark, or perhaps ask a parent or friend to mark it for you. This can be done by checking that you have any of the points, identified in the mark scheme, and listed under separate bullet points.

Final tips

Remember that most people do well in examinations when they learn the subject as it is taught. Very few students can do well by trying to revise the day before the examination, simply because, in most instances, there is too much work to go over and learn. Make your revision progressive and continuous rather than giving yourself a mountain to climb towards the end of the course. Try also to remember the following useful tips when you are about to revise:

- Draw up a revision timetable (plan) and mark on it precisely when you intend to revise for a subject, including the length of time to be devoted to revision.
- Find a space or a room that is comfortable, where there are no distractions and where you can concentrate on revising.
- Ensure that the room is warm but well ventilated.
- Revise for no more than 20–30 minutes at a time. Then take a brief rest, walk around, have a drink.
- It is far better to follow the above method than to try to spend long hours revising without any breaks.
- Revise at a time in the day that enables you to be attentive and concentrate properly. Late at night is rarely the best time for this.
- Check how much you know by asking a parent or friend to ask you questions on aspects of the theory. Believe it or not they do not need to know a great deal about the subject for this process to provide very useful feedback.
- Make a written note on any of the aspects or questions that constantly cause you difficulty and spend a little more time on them until you understand and remember them. Seek assistance from your teacher if you are unable to grasp a concept or understand specialist terminology.
- Remember that revision is something that you cannot do without fully concentrating on the topic in hand. If you feel that your concentration is wavering, you need a break.
- Finally, remember that time spent revising thoroughly and consistently should give you the confidence to go into the examination knowing that you are as well prepared as you possibly can be.

The skeleton and joints

What the skeleton does

blood
production

protection — connective
tissue
|
Skeleton — joints

movement — joints

shape and
support

Facts

The skeleton is the basic framework of the body.
The four basic functions of the skeleton are:

- shape and support
- movement
- protection
- blood production.

Key points

Shape and support
- The body would have no defined shape without the skeleton.
- The soft tissue organs are protected from damage by the skeleton's rigid frame.

Movement
- Movement is possible because the skeleton has joints.
- This occurs when the muscles attached to the bones contract and cause the joint to move; this is also known as articulation.
- Muscles use the skeleton to provide the leverage necessary for movement.
- The greatest movement occurs at the shoulder, elbow, wrist, neck, hip, knee and ankle.
- The least amount of movement occurs in the hands, feet and vertebrae.

Protection
- The skeleton provides protection for soft tissue organs such as the lungs, the heart, the spinal chord and the brain.
- Without this protection it would be impossible to undertake many day to day activities, including sports and recreations.

Blood production
- Plasma makes up just over half of blood volume.
- Red blood cells contain haemoglobin, which transport oxygen.
- White blood cells fight infection.
- Platelets assist in blood clotting.
- Blood production occurs in the bones of the skeleton, particularly the long bones of the arms and legs.

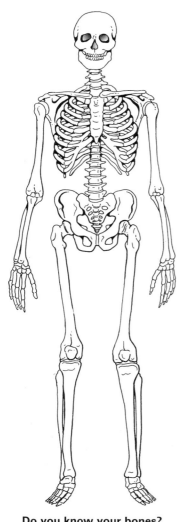

Do you know your bones?

Question

Identify the following bones on the illustration above: clavicle, humerus, ulna, radius, sternum, ribs, scapula, vertebra, pelvic bones, femur, tibia, fibula, carpals, metacarpals, tarsals, metatarsals, phalanges.

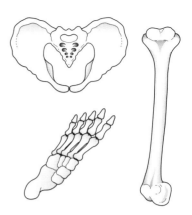

Types of bones

Facts

Bones are classified into three types or shapes:

- flat bones – e.g. the scapula, the pelvis and the ribs
- irregular bones – e.g. the bones of the hands and feet
- long bones – the bones of the arms and the legs.

 **points**

- Taller people have longer bones than short people.
- The sturdiness and size of bones influences overall body weight.

Joint structure

Facts

- Most moving joints are synovial joints.
- Connective tissue is a collective term, which may refer to:
  - cartilage
  - ligaments
  - tendons.

 **points**

Synovial joints
- Synovial joints are enclosed inside a capsule filled with fluid.
- Synovial fluid is a lubricant that reduces wear and friction at joint surfaces.
- A synovial joint can be any of the major joint types.

Cartilage
There are three types of cartilage found in the human body:
- yellow (or elastic) cartilage
- white fibro-cartilage
- hyaline (or blue/articular) cartilage.

Ligaments
- Ligaments are very strong, slightly elastic fibres.
- They bind bones together at joints and ensure that joints remain stable.
- Ligaments connect bone to bone.

Tendons
- Tendons are non-elastic fibres.
- They also help to stabilise joints.
- Tendons attach muscle to bone.

Did you know

That in infancy most of the skeleton is made up of cartilage, which turns into bone as we get older.

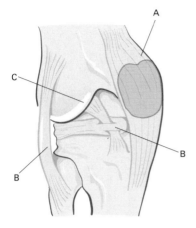

Questions

1. List two essential differences between ligaments and tendons.

2. What type of cartilage would you expect to find at the end of long bones?

3. Describe the role of:

   a) tendons at a joint

   b) ligaments at a joint.

4. In this diagram of a knee joint, identify which label (A, B or C) indicates ligament, cartilage and tendons.

Types of movement

Fact

Movement occurs when the ends of bones articulate at a joint as a result of muscular contraction.

 **points**

Particular movements identified by the OCR specification are:
- flexion or bending at a joint
- extension or straightening at a joint
- rotation at a joint
- abduction at a joint, causing movement away from the centre line of the body
- adduction at a joint, causing movement towards the centre line of the body.

Types of joint

Facts

- Movement is obtained at most of the body's joints.
- Some allow considerable movement, while others permit very little.
- This movement at joints is often referred to as articulation.
- Movement occurs when the ends of the bones articulate at a joint as a result of muscular contraction.

The OCR specification requires you to be familiar with the following types of joint:

- ball and socket joints
- hinge joints
- gliding joints
- pivot joints.

 **points**

Ball and socket joints
- Ball and socket joints permit the greatest range of movement.
- The 'ball' and 'socket' are held in place by ligaments and tendons.

Hinge joints
- Hinge joints allow extensive range of movement but in one plane only, i.e. very little rotation.
- This makes them susceptible to injury from twists and turns.

Gliding joints
- Gliding joints permit limited flexion/extension.
- These bones move or glide against each other.

Pivot joints
- An example is the head/neck joint.
- Pivot joints allow a good range of rotation, depression and elevation.

Questions

1. Give an example from a sporting or other physical activity of each of the five types of movement listed above.

2. Give an example of a ball and socket joint and describe its use in a sporting activity or physical skill.

3. Give an example of a sporting or physical skill in which a hinge joint plays a significant part.

4. Name two of the types of joint listed above that are also synovial joints.

Joints and performance

Facts
- Healthy joints are essential for free movement.
- Movement is influenced by the suppleness/strength of ligaments and tendons.
- Performance in sport is enhanced if joints are healthy and permit a good range of movement.
- Undue stretching or loading of joints is likely to produce serious injury.

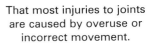 **points**

- Joints should not be stretched beyond a degree of minor discomfort.
- Joints should not be loaded (e.g. with weights), other than very gradually, beyond the working limits for which they have been prepared.
- The above is particularly important in young (physically immature) performers.

Did you know ?

That most injuries to joints are caused by overuse or incorrect movement.

focus point

Remember that the joints are the key to all movement. They should not be subjected to repeated, sudden and jarring shocks, nor stretched or contorted into positions for which they have not been especially prepared or intended. Although the skeleton is the framework for movement and protection, free movement cannot be obtained without healthy joints, ligaments and tendons.

- Synovial joints are found where considerable movement occurs and where loads tend to be greatest.
- Synovial fluid helps to reduce wear on these joints by acting as a lubricating agent.
- Ligaments and/or tendons can be damaged as a result of sudden twists and turns.

Questions

1. Why is the knee joint likely to be less stable than any of the other major joints of the body?

2. Why are some joints synovial joints, while others are not?

3. Which type of joints permit the greatest range of movement?

Key Words

Shape	Support
Movement	Protection
Blood production	Flat bones
	Irregular bones
Long bones	Synovial joints
Cartilage	
Ligaments	Tendons
Flexion	Extension
Rotation	Abduction
Adduction	Ball and socket joints
Hinge joints	Gliding joints
Pivot joints	

Exam tips

You need to understand:

- how the skeleton and joints relate both to each other and to their body systems
- the four major functions of the skeleton
- how different joints allow specific movements to take place
- how the skeleton and joints contribute to performance in a range of physical activities.

Muscles

The structure and function of muscle

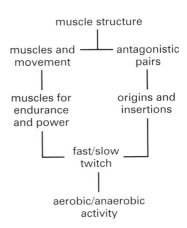

Facts

The body has three types of muscle:

- involuntary ('smooth') muscle
- cardiac (heart) muscle
- voluntary ('skeletal') muscle.

Key points

- Involuntary muscle is found in the body's internal organs and is not under our voluntary control.
- Cardiac muscle is found only in the heart; it is also involuntary and never stops working.
- Voluntary muscle is under our conscious control and enables movement to take place (e.g. flexing the biceps).

Did you know

That there are over 600 named muscles in the human body.

How muscles work

Facts

- All skeletal muscles have origins and insertions.
- These are the points at which muscles are attached to bones.
- Muscle groups work in pairs.
- One muscle is contracting while the other is relaxing.

Key points

- Some muscles have more than one point of attachment at either end.
- Origins are found at the end of the muscle, which remains fixed during movement.
- Insertions are found at the end of the muscle, which moves during movement.
- Muscular contractions shorten muscles so that the tendon at the point of insertion is pulled towards the point of origin.
- Muscles that work in pairs are called antagonistic pairs.
- The contracting muscle is known as the prime mover.
- The opposing muscle is known as the antagonist.
- Muscles that may assist in the movement are known as synergists.

Did you know

That 'antagonistic' means 'to work against' or 'to oppose'.

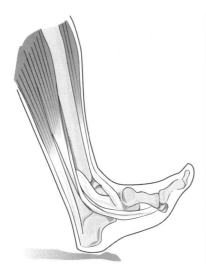

Questions

1. The diagram here shows the toes being raised towards the shin, an action involving the calf muscle and the frontal muscles of the lower leg. Identify which muscle is the prime mover in this movement.

2. Which muscle group would be the prime mover in bending the arm at the elbow joint?

3. Some physical activities require the raising of the arms above the head. Which muscle groups would be involved in this movement as prime mover and antagonist?

4. The quadriceps muscles play an important part in any kicking action. Which group of muscles would act as antagonists in such a movement?

5. In a tennis serve, one phase of the skill is sometimes described as 'throwing the head of the racquet at the ball'. Which group of muscles in the upper arm would initiate this action?

Muscles for endurance and power

Facts

- There are two types of muscle fibre present in all skeletal muscle: fast-twitch fibres and slow-twitch fibres.
- Anaerobic activity utilises energy stored within the muscles.
- Aerobic activity uses energy which can be replaced during exercise.

Key points

- Their names are an indication of the way each type of fibre works.
- Fast-twitch fibres contract very quickly and powerfully.
- Slow-twitch fibres contract less violently but can maintain this level of work for much longer periods.
- Fast-twitch fibres are for power and strength activities, in short bursts.
- Slow-twitch fibres are for endurance activities.
- Fast-twitch muscle fibres burn up their supply of oxygen very quickly, usually within ten seconds or less.
- Slow-twitch fibres can replace their oxygen supply while working and can continue to do so for an extended period.
- We cannot change the proportion of fast-twitch to slow twitch fibres through training.
- The distribution of fast-twitch to slow-twitch fibres is the same for all muscle groups.
- Although we can improve performance through training, we cannot increase our natural predisposition to be good at a particular type of activity.
- This means that although we may, for example, improve our sprinting speed, we can never be as good as someone who naturally has a much higher proportion of fast-twitch fibres in their muscles and who trains just as hard as we do.

focus point

In sudden or violent movement the prime mover muscles contract very strongly, exerting great force upon any attached tendons. This is one of the reasons why warm-up activity prior to competition is very important. Failure to address this necessity can cause serious tears or pulls to muscles, tendons or both.

Did you know

That the distribution of fast-twitch to slow-twitch muscle fibres is determined by heredity.

- Those individuals who are good at 'power' or 'explosive' events tend to have a high proportion of fast-twitch fibres.
- Those who excel in endurance events are usually found to have a higher than normal level of slow-twitch muscle fibres.
- Anaerobic exercise – without taking in oxygen; energy cannot be replaced without recovery.
- Aerobic exercise – utilises oxygen; energy can be replaced by utilising oxygen.
- Most team games involve both anaerobic and aerobic activity.

Did you know

That the only way we can discover just what percentage of fast-twitch to slow-twitch muscle fibres we have is under medical supervision.

Questions

1. Name three sporting or physical activities that only involve anaerobic exercise.
2. Name three sporting or physical activities that involve mainly aerobic exercise.

Muscles and performance

Facts

- Skeletal muscles become stronger the more they are used – this is known as hypertrophy.
- Reduction of activity or inactivity (e.g. through injury) causes muscles to become weaker and smaller – this is known as atrophy.

Key points

- Regular activity is essential to ensure muscular efficiency and health.
- Activity (or training) must be appropriate for the intended purpose.
- 'Off-season' exercise should be sufficient to maintain muscular efficiency.

The major muscle groups

Fact

Voluntary muscle is the basis of all intended movement.

Key points

The major muscle groups that the OCR specification requires you to know about are:
- deltoids
- trapezius
- pectorals
- biceps

focus point

The above differences may be less important in activities involving skill, co-ordination, teamwork and strategies. In individual activities where the sole criteria is athletic ability, the make-up of an individual's skeletal muscle may very well determine the potential limits of his or her level of performance. In team games and other activities involving high levels of co-operation and tactical awareness, it is less likely that pure athletic ability will be the major determining factor in the level of success achieved by a group or a team.

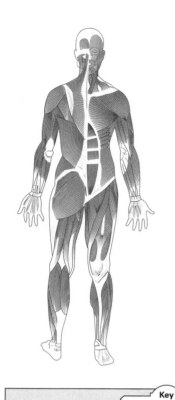

- triceps
- latissimus dorsi
- abdominals
- gluteals
- quadriceps
- hamstrings'
- gastrocnemius.

Questions

1. a) Do you know where the muscle groups listed above are to be found in the human body?

    b) Give examples of the type of movement produced by each of these muscle groups.

2. Give an example of the use of each muscle group in a specific physical or sporting activity.

3. Why are voluntary muscles so named?

4. Why is it inadvisable to completely stop activity during the 'close season'?

5. What is the difference between hypertrophy and atrophy?

Key Words

involuntary muscle	cardiac muscle
voluntary muscle	origins
prime mover	insertions
antagonist	synergist
slow-twitch fibres	fast-twitch fibres
aerobic	anaerobic
atrophy	hypertrophy
trapezius	deltoids
biceps	pectorals
latissimus dorsi	triceps
quadriceps	abdominals
gastrocnemius	gluteals
	hamstrings

Exam tips

You need to understand:

- that different types of muscle fibres perform in different ways
- how the muscular system relates to other body systems
- how activity and exercise develop the strength and efficiency of muscles
- that muscles function in different ways in order to enable movement to take place.

The circulatory and respiratory systems

Getting oxygen to the muscles

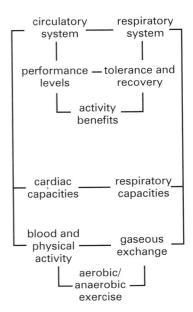

Facts

- The heart pumps blood around the body via the arteries.
- Blood is returned to the heart via the veins.

 **points**

- Arteries and veins become smaller the further they are from the heart.
- These smaller vessels are known as arterioles and venules.
- The smallest vessels of all are known as capillaries.
- Circulating blood carries nutrients and oxygen to the muscles and waste products to be excreted.
- Oxygenated blood is pumped to the muscles.
- Deoxygenated blood returns to the heart and is pumped to the lungs, where it is reoxygenated.
- The circulatory and respiratory systems must work together.
- Circulation and respiration can both be improved through regular activity and/or training.

Circulation and respiration: participation and performance

Facts

High levels of physical activity raise several issues relating to:

- lactic acid
- duration
- gradually increasing the intensity and/or durability of physical activity.
- oxygen debt
- recovery rate

 **points**

Lactic acid
- Lactic acid build-up prevents muscles from working efficiently.
- This occurs far more quickly in activities requiring all-out effort.

Oxygen debt
- This occurs when the rate at which muscles are required to work is greater than the rate at which the body can take in oxygen.
- Oxygen debt creates a shortage of oxygen and muscle fatigue.

Duration

- Fatigue develops much more gradually in activities of longer duration and less intensity.

Recovery rate

- Recovery from anaerobic activity occurs much more quickly than from extended aerobic activity.

Tolerance

- It is possible to increase the tolerance to lactic acid and oxygen debt by gradually increasing the intensity/duration of activity.

Benefits of exercise: the circulatory system

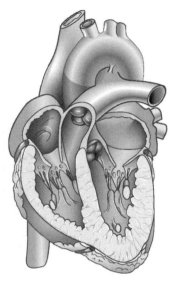

The heart beats approximately 40 million times in one year

Fact
Regular exercise makes cardiac muscle stronger and enlarges the heart.

 **points**

Stronger cardiac muscle

- The heart muscle becomes stronger as a result of regular exercise.

Increased stroke volume

- The amount of blood pumped from the heart during a single beat.
- The greater the stroke volume, the greater the amount of blood that is pumped around the body for each heartbeat.

Increased cardiac output

- The total volume of blood pumped from the heart during one minute (output = stroke volume x beats per minute).

Lower resting heart rate

- Because the heart pumps more blood around the body each time it beats, it works far more efficiently.
- As fitness increases, resting heart rate decreases.

Improving performance: the respiratory system

Fact
The process of gaseous exchange involves both the respiratory and circulatory systems.

 **points**

- Gaseous exchange involves the exchange of oxygen and carbon dioxide between the bloodstream and the lungs.

- Oxygen is absorbed into, and CO_2 is dispersed from, the bloodstream via the microporous walls of the alveoli.
- The process occurs far more efficiently in individuals who take regular exercise.
- The efficiency with which gaseous exchange occurs governs the body's ability to make the best use of oxygen intake and expel waste products.

Questions

1. What is the difference between blood that is being pumped out of the heart and blood that is returning to the heart?

2. Why does lactic acid accumulate more rapidly during anaerobic exercise?

3. What is the difference between stroke volume and cardiac output?

4. Describe briefly the process of gaseous exchange.

Benefits from exercise

Fact

Regular exercise has a beneficial effect on the respiratory system.

 **points**

Increased vital capacity
- Vital capacity is the total volume of air you can move into and out of the lungs in one deep breath.

Tidal volume
- Tidal volume is the amount of air passing through the lungs while at rest.
- An increase in tidal volume is usually an indicator of increased vital capacity.

Oxygen debt tolerance
- Increases in both the oxygen-carrying capacity of the blood and the vital capacity of the lungs allow the body to tolerate oxygen debt during exercise.

The blood and physical activity

Facts

Blood has three primary functions:
- transport
- protection
- regulation.

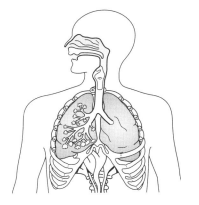

The respiratory system

Did you know

That there are approximately six litres of blood in the human body.

focus point

Blood doing its job:

- blood carries digested foods and hormones in addition to oxygen, and carries away waste products including carbon dioxide

- red blood cells carry oxygen to where the body needs it

- white blood cells kill bacteria and make some damaging substances harmless

- blood platelets are cell fragments that enable the blood to clot.

Did you know

That the body automatically switches to aerobic activity when it reaches the anaerobic threshold.

focus point

Team games have a particular requirement for most participants to work continually (aerobically) but with frequent 'flat out' bursts of anaerobic activity. Although the duration and level of aerobic activity can be improved by training, this is not the case for anaerobic exercise. However, appropriate training can improve the time it takes to recover from working at maximum levels and this should be the focus for this aspect of training programmes for players of team games.

 **points**

Transport

- Blood transports oxygen from the lungs to the muscles and carbon dioxide back to the lungs.

Protection

- Blood contains clotting agents.
- White blood cells protect us from infection.

Regulation

- Blood helps to regulate the body's temperature – the veins and capillaries near to the skin expand or contract in response to heat or cold.

Aerobic and anaerobic activity

Fact

The amount of work the body can do is limited by its capacity to replace the energy it uses.

 **points**

- Some physical activities/sports involve both aerobic and anaerobic forms of exercise.
- Training programmes must accommodate any requirement to switch between aerobic and anaerobic exercise.

Aerobic activity

- In aerobic activity oxygen intake must exceed the rate at which it is being used.
- The removal of lactic acid must also exceed the rate at which it accumulates.
- These limits can be considerably increased as a result of appropriate training.

Anaerobic activity

- Anaerobic activity involves working without oxygen.
- Such activity utilises energy stored in the muscles.
- This type of activity can be sustained for only a few seconds.
- Recovery from anaerobic activity is much more rapid than recovery from aerobic work.

Questions

1. Why is the efficiency with which blood is transported around the body important to physically active people?

2. Why is it important that games players improve their ability to recover from anaerobic activity?

Exam tips

You need to understand:

- how these systems affect participation and performance in practical activities
- how activity and exercise develop the efficiency of the circulatory and respiratory systems, particularly the heart, lungs and blood composition
- the essential parts of the above systems and the changes that result from exercise
- the difference between aerobic and anaerobic work and the effect of lactic acid on performance.

Key Words

arteries	veins
arterioles	venules
capillaries	oxygenated
deoxygenated	lactic acid
oxygen debt	recovery rate
tolerance	heart rate
stroke	cardiac
volume	output
gaseous	vital
exchange	capacity
tidal volume	transport
protection	regulation
aerobic	anaerobic
recovery	anaerobic threshold

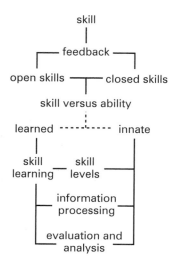

Skill

What is skill?

> **Facts**
>
> Skill has been defined as:
>
> *The learned ability to bring about predetermined results with maximum certainty, often with the minimum outlay of time or energy or both.* (Guthrie, 1956)

 **Key points**

- A skill is learned.
- It should become predictable, consistent and efficient.

Feedback

> **Facts**
>
> Feedback is information received by a performer either during or after a performance. The four types of feedback are:
>
> - intrinsic feedback
> - extrinsic feedback
> - knowledge of performance (KP)
> - knowledge of results (KR).

 **Key points**

Intrinsic feedback

- Intrinsic feedback comes from within the performance.
- You need to be experienced to be able to utilise intrinsic feedback.

Extrinsic feedback

- Extrinsic feedback comes from others (e.g. teacher or coach).
- Whether general or specific, it should be brief (one or two points) so as not to be confusing.
- Extrinsic feedback needs to be given either during a performance or soon afterwards.

Knowledge of performance (KP)

- This can be intrinsic, but it is most likely to come from an external source (e.g. coach or video analysis).
- It involves analysing the nature of a performance and working out how it may be improved.
- The results are not important – even a successful performance can be improved.

Knowledge of results (KR)

- This comes from an external source, e.g. as a result of a game (football) or the judges' score (gymnastics).
- It is a useful form of feedback where results might indicate the cause of poor performance.

Open and closed skills

Open skills	Closed skills
passing	'set piece' skills
tackling	shot putt
striking	tennis serve
kicking	pole vault
catching	trampolining

> **Fact**
>
> Whether a skill is open or closed is determined by the environment in which it takes place and the degree to which the performer needs to respond to any changes.

 **points**

Closed skills

- Closed skills require little or no adjustment during performance.
- Once learnt they remain essentially the same (habitual).
- They may require a great deal of practice to perfect them.
- The environment is relatively stable.

Open skills

- Open skills need to be constantly adapted during performance.
- The performance environment may change (perceptual).
- Team games require open skills.

Skill and ability

> **Facts**
>
> Ability is innate – which means that we are born with it. Some individuals are naturally faster, better co-ordinated, more artistic or have greater mathematical ability than others.

 **points**

- Speed – the ability of a performer to move quickly.
- Reaction time – the speed of response to a stimulus; reaction time and speed of movement are linked.
- Agility – the ability to move quickly, and control and change the point of balance.
- Co-ordination – the ability to control and link different movements in a sequence or skill.
- Flexibility – the ability to stretch and bend to maximise the range of movement at joints.

focus point

Was Michael Owen born with the ability to be a great footballer? Are his football skills the result of excellent coaching, or might there be another reason?

● Balance – the ability to maintain balance when moving or standing still.

Questions

1. Watch a friend perform an activity and identify two pieces of information that you think will help to significantly improve his or her performance.

2. Identify two closed skills and two open skills from your own practical activities.

3. Explain why a forehand groundstroke in tennis is an open skill.

4. Explain the difference between skill and ability.

Different levels of skill

skill levels
|
cognitive
|
associative
|
autonomous

Facts

● The performance of a novice is very different from that of a top-level performer.
● Development occurs gradually and involves much hard work.

Key points

● The novice may well be:
  ■ inconsistent – performing a skill differently each time.
  ■ inefficient in energy expenditure and ineffective as a performer
  ■ unable to perform a skill quickly, e.g. may be caught in possession
  ■ unable to adapt a skill, e.g. a novice batsman who is bowled out because he is unable to adapt his stroke.
● The top-level performer will:
  ■ demonstrate a high level of consistency
  ■ perform with apparently little energy or effort
  ■ perform a skill quickly and efficiently
  ■ adapt skills to meet the demands of a situation.
● Key words to remember:
  ■ consistency
  ■ energy
  ■ time
  ■ adaptability.

Did you know ❓

That early improvements in skill usually level out. This is known as a performance plateau.

Facts

In order to learn or improve skills a performer must take part in coaching or teaching sessions and practice.

Learning and developing skill

 points

Simple skills – whole learning

- Simple skills can be learned as a whole unit.

Complex skills – part learning

- Some skills need to be broken down into smaller parts ('mini-skills'), e.g. a 'lay up' in basketball could be broken down into dribble, pick-up, lay-up strides, jump and release.
- When these mini-skills have been perfected they can be joined together as a whole skill.

Demonstration and copying

- Skills are learned by copying others who provide a good technical model.
- A demonstration should be followed by immediate feedback on the student's performance.
- Live or video performance can be used to demonstrate ideal technique.

Practice

- 'Perfect practice makes perfect' – skills become 'grooved' as a result of practice.
- A good demonstration is essential.
- Opportunities for both intrinsic and extrinsic feedback must be available.
- Practice can be based on a whole skill or a part of a skill (mini-skill).

Trial and error

- Trial and error means doing something until you happen to hit on a way that makes it work.
- Bad habits can be picked up, which can be difficult to break later.

Role models

- Stars in a particular sport can be very useful in demonstrating skills.
- The role model needs to be technically good.
- A good role model will also promote sporting values in their conduct both on and off the field.

learning/developing skills
- simple skills – whole learning
- complex skills – part learning

demonstration
copying
practice
trial and error
role models

focus point

It is important not to confuse simple and complex skills with open and closed skills – they are entirely different ways of categorising skills.

Learning skills: information processing

Fact

When we are learning skills and/or performing them during competition, we are constantly processing information.

 points

Input

- The performer considers 'what is happening?' – it might be the flight and speed of a shuttlecock and/or the position of an opponent.

information processing

input → decision-making → output

feedback

Did you know

That new skills only remain in the short-term memory for around two minutes, unless they are repeated regularly.

- The performer constantly receives information to do with the pitch, an opponent, how the wind might affect performance, etc.

Decision-making

- Based on the above, and on previous experience, the performer must decide on how to respond; what stroke to play; where, and how quickly to move; whether to pass or dribble.

Output

- This is executing a decision as a result of the above, e.g. deciding to play a top-spin lob, having noticed that your opponent is 'rushing the net'.

Feedback

- Having performed the selected skill, the performer will receive information about it.
- Types of feedback are intrinsic/extrinsic feedback, knowledge of results (KR) and knowledge of performance (KP).
- This information will be added to that already stored in the memory and should influence any future decisions if a similar situation occurs again.

Evaluation and analysis

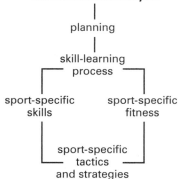

Fact

Performance skills can only be improved if you know what is wrong with them and how this might be put right.

 **points**

Evaluation and analysis

- This means watching a performance and identifying what is good and bad.
- This might refer to skills, tactics or fitness.
- This might involve attack or defence, or an individual skill.

Planning

- It is important to plan for improvement.
- What can be done to improve a performance, and how?

Skill-learning process

- The provider of feedback needs to know how relevant skills are learned and improved.

Sport-specific skills

- The provider of feedback should have detailed knowledge of the skills under scrutiny.
- These might be group/team skills or individual skills.

Sport-specific fitness

- The provider of feedback must have activity-specific fitness knowledge.

Sport-specific tactics and strategies

- The provider of feedback must know about the specific tactics and strategies of the game or activity.

Questions

1. Draw and label a simple information processing model including the arrows.

2. Redraw the above model, but this time fit it into a sporting scenario of your choice.

3. How might feedback from an élite performance differ from that of a novice?

4. Select a simple skill and a complex skill and describe how you would teach them to a novice.

focus point

All this information should come from good feedback. It therefore needs to come from someone who has specialised knowledge and, most importantly, is able to communicate such information effectively.

Key Words

feedback	intrinsic
extrinsic	knowledge of
knowledge	performance
of results	(KP)
(KR)	open skill
closed skill	ability
agility	co-ordination
flexibility	balance
reaction time	level of skill
consistency	energy
time	adaptability
learning	simple skills
complex	whole
skills	learning
part learning	demonstration
copying	practice
trial and	role models
error	information
input	processing
decision-	output
making	evaluation
analysis	planning
skill-learning	sport-specific
process	skills
sport-specific	sport-specific
fitness	tactics and
	strategies

Motivation and mental preparation

Mental preparation

mental preparation

- relaxation
- mental rehearsal
- focusing

goal setting

> **Fact**
>
> In modern top-level sport where performers are often equally matched in terms of skill and fitness, mental preparation is extremely important.

 **points**

Relaxation

- The mind and the body are very closely linked, so relaxation should involve both physical and mental relaxation.
- Physical relaxation utilises massage and manipulation techniques to reduce the muscular tension that builds up before a big match or competition.
- Mental relaxation is achieved in different ways, e.g. by playing calming music, meditation, quiet talking with a coach or friend or going for a walk.
- The term 'self-talk' is used to describe the performer going through a prepared routine of self-communication, both prior to and during competition.

Mental rehearsal

- Mental imagery is the ability to picture what a skill should look like when performed well (a useful tool in the learning process).
- It is used in preparation for big competitions where performers picture specific skills or key aspects of the performance.
- This can build up a performer's confidence.

Focusing

- This involves focusing on the key points of a technique and key tactical ideas.
- The performer should be free from distractions.

What is motivation?

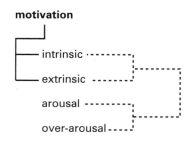

> **Fact**
>
> Motivation is the desire to perform well.

Intrinsic motivation

- This is self-motivation and involves:
  - a desire to participate for our own personal reasons
  - a desire to participate for fun and fitness
  - enjoying playing with friends or as part of a team.

Extrinsic motivation

- Extrinsic motivation comes from outside our own personal drives.
- It involves:
  - winning cups, trophies and medals
  - high salaries and prize money
  - personal glory, fame and status.

Arousal

- This is a state of readiness in a performer.
- Motivation is an effective way of stimulating arousal.
- Coaches/captains 'psyching up' their team before a match.
- Cup finals, prize money, gold medals and media contracts are guaranteed to raise arousal levels.

Over-arousal

- Some performers are all too easily aroused – this can cause problems!
- Mike Tyson has a reputation for 'losing it', ear-biting and, more recently, fighting at a pre-contest promotion with Lennox Lewis.

focus point

Coaches, teachers and sport governing bodies use a range of extrinsic motivators in order to generate and promote interest in a whole range of sporting activities. For most people participation is the result of a mixture of intrinsic and extrinsic influences.

Goal setting

> **Fact**
>
> This is a process whereby achievable goals are agreed by you and your teacher/coach in order to improve your performance.

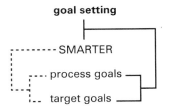

goal setting — SMARTER, process goals, target goals

 **Key points**

SMARTER

- **S** Specific – goals must be clear and precise.
- **M** Measurable – there should be a standard against which progress can be measured.
- **A** Accepted – the goal is agreed by performer and coach.
- **R** Realistic – goals or targets must be realistically achievable.
- **T** Time-related – a specific time span gives added focus.
- **E** Exciting – motivating and interesting.
- **R** Recorded – progress should be measured and recorded.

Types of goal

- There are two main types of goals: process goals and target goals.
- Process goals:
  - Process goals usually relate to an aspect of performance.
  - This might be a specific technique or skill or adjustments to a tactical approach.
  - A sprinter who is slow out of the blocks, or a games player who is slow off the mark, might logically set a process goal related to the improvement of explosive speed or acceleration.
- Target goals:
  - Target goals identify specific targets in overall performance.
  - This might be an 800m runner wanting to improve a personal best performance by a specific amount, or a cricketer wanting to improve his or her batting average.

> **Did you know ?**
>
> That the setting of unrealistic or impossible goals is demotivating to a performer.

focus point

Setting achievable goals breaks performance improvement down into manageable, less threatening chunks. This helps to increase motivation and reduce anxiety. Remember, it is easier to work towards lots of smaller goals than it is to work towards one big goal, which may be years in the future.

Key Words

mental preparation
relaxation
mental rehearsal
focusing
goal setting
motivation
intrinsic motivation
extrinsic motivation
arousal
over-arousal
goal-setting
SMARTER
process goals
target goals

Questions

1. For a sport of your choice and using the information on mental preparation as a guide, design a pre-performance routine to fully prepare your performer for competition.

2. What is the difference between intrinsic and extrinsic motivation?

3. How would you reduce the likelihood of over-arousal in a performer who suffers from this problem?

4. Are there any dangers or problems with participating for extrinsic reasons?

5. Select one athletic event and a specific position in a team game and for each scenario identify a realistic process and target goal. Assume the performer to be an average Year 9 student.

6. With a friend, use the SMARTER principles to negotiate some goals that might help to improve performance in one of your chosen activities.

Exam tips

You need to understand:

- how motivation and mental preparation affect practical performance
- how different types of mental preparation affect practical performance
- the difference between intrinsic and extrinsic motivation and how they can affect performance
- the importance of goal setting as part of mental preparation, as a means of controlling anxiety and as a way of motivating performers.

Social reasons for participation

Increased leisure time

Facts

Ordinary people now have far more leisure time than ever before. Reasons include:

- the shorter working week
- early retirement
- technological advances
- unemployment.

 **points**

The shorter working week

- Many people now work 37 hours or less.
- Many people work part time.
- Flexible shift patterns and extended weekends often provide large periods of recreation time.

Technological advances

- These have contributed to a shorter working week.
- Many people can now work from home.
- Wide ownership of personal transport allows a more effective use of leisure time.
- Negative aspects of technological advances include:
  - work is far less physically demanding
  - unemployment
  - a more sedentary lifestyle
  - effects on general levels of health fitness.

Early retirement

- Retirement allows an increasingly large group of people the freedom and opportunity to pursue new or existing recreational pursuits.
- Many retired and early retired groups have far more disposable income than previous generations.

Unemployment

- Unemployment creates 'free time' which can be used for affordable recreation.
- Unemployment is sometimes brought about (ironically) as a result of technological changes that have increased recreational opportunities for others.

Why people participate

Facts

There are many reasons why people take part in sport and/or physical activities. These include:

- health
- leisure and enjoyment
- vocation.

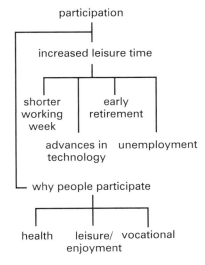

 Did you know

That in the very near future approximately forty per cent of the population will be retired people.

focus point

It is ironic that the development of new technologies has contributed to the enhancement of the lifestyle of many people, whilst at the same time contributing to the unemployment of others. Similarly, whilst unemployment provides a temporary opportunity for additional recreation, it also takes away the means of making the best use of such time. Other than in the majority of élite sports, it should not be assumed that those who do participate in physical activities are predominantly young people.

Health

- There is an increasing level of concern about health.
- Many people exercise in order to avoid stress.
- Many jobs involve little or no physical activity, so that regular exercise ensures a reasonable level of fitness.
- Some people use exercise to aid recovery from illness or injury.
- Some people are concerned about their physical image.

Leisure and enjoyment

- Many people participate in physical activity simply because they enjoy it.
- The right to recreation has become the norm in most free societies, irrespective of class or privilege.
- Friendships develop through recreational and/or sporting experiences.
- Leisure (or enjoyment) is no longer considered frivolous or a waste of time.
- For some people, physical recreation serves as an extension to social activity.
- Physical activities or recreations can also be hobbies.
- Enjoyment of physical activity may or may not include activity of a sporting or competitive nature.
- The recent increase in popularity of gyms and health clubs also provides an indication that exercise and fitness are now seen as important. It has become fashionable to be fit!

Vocation

- There are those who are professional performers and others who have careers as coaches, fitness trainers, physiotherapists, and recreational and sports development officers.
- PE teachers have traditionally been one of a very few professional groups paid to teach sport.
- Some sports have part-time professionals who also have full- or part-time jobs.
- Many clubs now have full-time secretaries, commercial managers and administrative staff.
- Organisations such as UK Sport, Sport England and other sports bodies employ support staff.

Questions

1. Give three reasons why leisure time has increased.
2. Why is it likely that older people will have more influence on recreation in the future?

Key Words

leisure
vocational
flexible shift patterns
technological advances
disposable income
sedentary lifestyle
stress
the right to recreation
frivolous

Exam tips

You need to understand:

- why people participate in physical activities
- the social and other factors that affect participation
- the reasons for increases in leisure time for some groups of people
- the health benefits that accrue from participation in physical activities

School

Promoters of physical activity

> **Fact**
>
> Schools play an important part in promoting and encouraging participation in sport and physical activity.

 **points**

The National Curriculum

- The National Curriculum was created by the government.
- It tells state schools what they have to teach from primary school until the end of Year 11.
- It sets out aims, standards and range of activity guidelines in physical education, such as in games, dance, swimming, athletics, outdoor adventurous activities and gymnastics.
- Active participation is essential for skill development.
- It also teaches vital information about health, lifestyle and working with others.

Examination courses

- GCSE, GNVQ, AS, A2, NVQ and Btech courses are available in Physical Education.
- There are also degree courses available in Physical Education, Sport and Leisure and Recreation.
- These courses and qualifications open up related career paths.
- PE examination combines theory and practical work and, like normal PE, must meet National Curriculum requirements.

Extra-curricular activities

- These are activities that take place in addition to National Curriculum requirements – usually out of school time – during lunchtimes, after school, at weekends or during school holidays.
- They include house/school teams, recreational clubs, skiing and sports trips, Duke of Edinburgh and Sports Leaders awards.
- Schools often organise their own competitions and/or link up with sports governing bodies that promote sport at local, district, county, national and international levels.
- Tens of thousands of young people benefit from their early experiences in school sports and recreations – activities that often remain part of their lives for many years afterwards.

Links with local clubs and sports providers

- Sporting links are developed in a variety of ways.
- Teachers and parents may be members of clubs and encourage young people to join.

Did you know

That PE is one of the fastest growing examination subjects.

Did you know ❓

That, for many young people, the sports they take up at school become lifelong interests.

- Schools often make use of off-site facilities for squash, swimming or rock climbing, helping to introduce students to recreational opportunities available in their local community and elsewhere.
- A school trip or a link with a local sailing club may stimulate a lifelong interest.
- It is now common practice for school facilities to be made available to local clubs, and an increasing number of school sports facilities are utilised as community sports centres.
- A network of Schools Sports Co-ordinators based in sports colleges has recently been created, with responsibility for developing links between schools and outside sporting organisations.

Questions

1. Write a paragraph to describe the effect of the National Curriculum on school Physical Education.

2. What is meant by the term 'extra-curricular activities'?

3. List any links with local clubs and sports providers that you are aware exist with your school.

Exam tips

You need to understand:

- the importance of physical activity to personal health, social and mental health, and physical well-being
- the role of the school in promotion participation in physical activity
- the importance and purpose of the National Curriculum in physical education
- about other local activities and facilities which are promoted through physical education in school.

Key Words

National Curriculum
examination courses
extra-curricular activities
sporting links

Social background

Positive and negative influences on participation

> **Fact**
>
> Attitudes to all kinds of physical activity are almost wholly the result of social and cultural influences.

🔑 Key points

Access

- Whilst for many people wide-ranging sporting and recreational facilities are becoming more commonplace, there are still those for whom provision is either limited or non-existent.
- Access to recreation is limited by free time and the nature (or amount) of facility provision.
- Access can be restricted or improved as a result of personal wealth (or lack of it).
- Levels of public or municipal provision greatly influence the degree of access available to ordinary people.
- The degree to which existing facilities are available for 'multi-use' (e.g. sports facilities in schools) also affects levels of access for a number of different social groups.
- The role of local authorities in the provision of facilities for grass-roots sport and recreation is critically important.
- Some groups, including ethnic minorities, the aged, disability groups and those in deprived areas, are still less likely to have the same access to facilities as more mainstream groups.
- Some facilities, including swimming and other water-based activities, are very expensive to build and operate.
- Some facilities are private and access is limited to those who can afford high membership and subscription fees.
- The important issues for most people are:
  - what is local?
  - what is available?
  - what is affordable?

Age

- The number of older people in the population is growing rapidly and this will influence the nature of facility provision in the future.
- Older people have not previously figured in plans for facility provision.
- Older people are becoming increasingly aware of the benefits of active recreation in terms of health and well-being.
- Many people who are currently retired are far better off financially than previous generations of old people.
- Older people are no longer prepared to accept that active recreations are not for them.

---

social background

positive influences — negative influences

- access
- age
- disability
- education
- environment/climate
- family
- gender
- media
- peer group
- politics
- poverty
- sponsorship
- tradition/culture

---

focus point

Access is about the freedom of individuals and groups to participate in sports and recreations. Poverty, disability, age and gender are just some of the reasons for restricted access. No one should be denied access to sport and/or recreation purely because someone else decides that this should be the case.

Did you know

That clubs catering for veteran sports are among the fastest growing organisations in the UK.

- Society is being forced to change its views on older people and active recreations.

Disability

- Athletes with disability – not disabled athletes!
- Disability sport – not disabled sport!
- Disability sport has fought an uphill battle against lack of provision for its athletes.
- Society used to hold the view that disabled people had no need to take part in sport and recreation.
- In the last 20 years disability sport has grown rapidly and forced society to change its views.
- Disability sport is now accepted as a valid form of physical activity.

Education

- The most obvious contribution education can make is in encouraging young people to take up activities while they are young.
- As an increasing number of young people continue their education beyond the age of 16, colleges and universities can play an increasingly significant part in promoting active recreations.
- Adult education classes, the youth service, and other youth organisations offer classes and/or provide facilities for recreational and sporting activities.
- Education also helps to form and reinforce attitudes to participation.
- It is also a process that teaches young people about shared responsibility, equality of opportunity and the tolerance of cultural differences.
- Physical activity in schools is important as it influences future lifetime habits.
- There are current issues that adversely affect the ability of schools to provide such opportunities and experiences, such as:
  - playing fields being sold off by local authorities
  - PE time being reduced to allow increased time for other subjects
  - reduced staffing to cut costs
  - teachers who are so busy that they have less time to give to extra-curricular activities.

Did you know

That the English Schools Athletics Championships held each July is the largest such festival in the world?

Questions

1. Name three factors which affect the link between access to sporting facilities and levels of participation?

2. Give two reasons why education is an important factor in sport and/or recreation?

Environment/climate

- The physical environment in which people live has a significant effect on the nature of their sports and recreations.
- In some parts of the world, the climate is so extreme that certain activities (e.g. winter sports) develop very strongly.
- At the same time, many other activities are simply not sustainable.

- Physical features (e.g. extended coastline or rugged mountainous terrain) encourage certain activities which cannot be practised in areas not possessing these features.
- Britain has an extensive coastline so that sailing has always been popular; this is also the case in France and other countries whose boundaries include extensive coastlines.
- Technology now allows some sporting environments to be created artificially, making it possible for some activities to take place in areas where they could not normally do so.
- The point above does not apply to those countries who simply cannot afford to take advantage of such developments.
- The most popular sports in most cultures (at non-élite level) are those that take place in their natural environment.
- In the UK we live on an island that has a temperate climate capable of sustaining many sports and recreations.
- We do not, however, normally have summers that will allow uninterrupted summer sports, nor winters that will support, for example, a sustained winter sports season, as is the case in some other European countries.

Family

- For many young people, their earliest sporting experiences occur within a family environment.
- Parental or extended family involvement in sport can be a major influence on young people.
- It is more common for one or both parents to be able to find time to actively support their children's participation in sport.
- Family holidays are sometimes based on sporting/recreational activities in which all are involved.
- Young people growing with positive experiences are more likely to develop an interest in such activities themselves.
- Even where there is no direct parental involvement, any interest shown in their children's activities has a positive effect on how young people feel about their own participation.
- Where parents give little support, it is less likely that an interest in sport will develop unless other factors (e.g. school or friends) exert a more positive influence.

Gender

- In most cultures, the argument that girls and women belong in the home and have no place on the sports field is no longer considered valid.
- Former excuses included 'they aren't strong enough' or 'it just isn't ladylike'.
- Girls and women now participate in activities previously considered to be suitable only for men.
- In most cultures, women no longer need 'male permission' to participate in sport and recreation.
- Significant obstacles still exist in some cultures, largely because of religious and/or political beliefs.
- There remains a more general objection to women's participation in certain activities (e.g. boxing).

positive influences
- family holidays
- parents or other family members involved in sport
- being taken to sporting events
- family membership, e.g. tennis club
- parents or other family members coming to watch you play
- being encouraged to enjoy it – even if you don't win!
- knowing that sport is valued

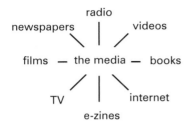

- Where young girls (or boys) are concerned, the issue should be whether boxing is a desirable activity.

The media

- Today's media exerts a greater influence than ever on sport.
- TV companies exert a major influence on major sporting events in order to market their advertisers' products.
- Sports stars now have a very high profile and exert a more powerful influence as role models than some pop stars.
- The nature of media coverage can influence public opinion on sport-related topics.
- The abundance of printed and electronic media means that few do not come into regular contact with media reportage.
- Much of this is not necessarily the kind of exposure that sports organisations would prefer, but it does ensure that sport has a very high profile, which can act as a spur to people to become involved in sport themselves.

Peer group

- Peer group pressure is a major factor in the lifestyles of young people, who are strongly influenced by the interests and activities of their friends.
- It takes considerable strength of character to refuse to just 'follow the crowd'.
- Many of today's leisure-time activities centre around the television, computer games or pop music, none of which are ideal ways to promote a healthy lifestyle.

Politics

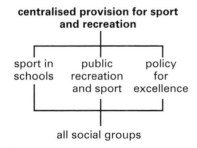

- The 1960s saw the emergence of Eastern European athletes who were almost unbeatable.
- One of the ways in which they had become successful was by ensuring that everyone had an opportunity to play games and sports from a very early age.
- This was possible because of direct (central) government funding.
- France was the first western European country to copy this centralised approach.
- This is often referred to as mass participation or Sport for All.
- Most other countries, including Britain and the USA, had rather haphazard systems of sports facility provision (i.e. de-centralised approach).
- These systems involved little or no government funding.
- Funding from the National Lottery and the restructuring of the UK's sports councils have begun to have some effect.
- Many decisions on the nature of facility provision are still taken at local level.
- Political views can influence the nature of provision within any given country.
- In the former Soviet Union, everything was funded by the state and financed by the revenue from taxes.
- In the USA, sport and recreation is funded only minimally by state and/or federal authorities.

- In many countries, funding and facilities are provided by a mixture of government, private and sometimes voluntary (or charitable) organisations.

Poverty

- Poverty can affect whole countries or particular areas.
- Where poverty exists, individuals, families and communities may well have other priorities than recreation or sport.
- Governments in very poor countries (e.g. Argentina and Kenya) find it almost impossible to make any provision for sport at any level.
- In the UK, the Active Communities programme, sponsored by Sport England, encourages deprived and ethnic minority groups to apply for funding in order to develop facilities locally.

Did you know

That in the whole of Africa only 7 per cent of schools have proper PE facilities.

Sponsorship

- Sponsorship is 'the funding of sporting activity for commercial gain'.
- The Institute of Sports Sponsorship is now jointly responsible with the Central Council of Physical Recreation (CCPR) for sponsorship matters in the UK.
- Together, they form the Sports Sponsorship Advisory Service (SSAS).
- The purpose of the SSAS is to develop sport by means of commercial sponsorship.
- One of the products of this relationship is Sportsmatch, which encourages grass-roots sport by doubling any amount raised locally by sporting organisations.
- The Active Communities Development Fund is another scheme designed to help particularly those groups in socially deprived areas to provide facilities where none exist.
- Some corporate sponsorship helps grass-roots sport.
- Much of the funding from sponsorship goes straight to professional sports and does not always reach sport at grass-roots level.

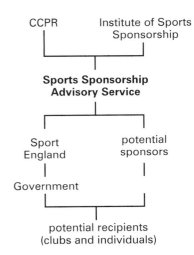

Tradition and culture

- Tradition and culture have been the foundation of most sports and also the cause of access being denied to many people.
- Cultures and traditions change, and the way that sport is perceived will also change with them.
- Ancient games and festivals have produced the basis of most of today's sports.
- Games and sports change with the cultures in which they exist.
- The raucous 'mob' games of nineteenth-century England were either constrained or banned by a strict Victorian morality.
- This Victorian morality also looked down on professional sport and promoted the values of amateur competition.
- In many cultures women have been consistently denied access to sport and physical recreation.
- The first Islamic Women's Games was held as recently as 1993.
- 27 countries did not send women competitors to the Olympic Games in 1996; by 2000 this had fallen to 9 countries.
- Cultural traditions and values differ markedly in different parts of the world, and this includes attitudes to sport.

Did you know ?

That the game of football was played in China over 2000 years ago.

Key Words

access
disability
environment/
  climate
media
poverty
tradition/
  culture
provision
grass-roots
opportunity
active
  recreation
encouraging
participation
tolerance
cultures
physical
  features
support
role models
peer group
  pressure
Eastern
  European
Sport for All
priorities
Sportsmatch
constrained

age
education
family
gender
politics
sponsorship
participate
influence
municipal
  provision
health
lack of
  provision
promoting
responsibility
experiences
extreme
technology
natural
obstacles
public
  opinion
'follow the
  crowd'
government
  funding
SSAS
corporate

Questions

1. Give two examples of climate or terrain influencing sporting activity in a particular area.

2. How can peer group pressure act as a demotivator to young people to take part in sport?

3. Why are there still objections to the participation of women and girls in some sports?

4. Explain why facilities for minority groups are more likely to be provided by central government funding than by private enterprise.

5. Name one initiative designed to help people in deprived areas develop sports facilities in their own locality in the UK.

6. Define the term 'sponsorship'.

Exam tips

You need to understand:

- how the range of facilities and opportunities affect participation in different physical activities
- how age, gender, access and education can have both positive and negative effects on participation
- how social factors such as the family, peer group and disability can have positive and negative influences on participation
- the effects that the media, sponsorship, politics and tradition/culture can have on participation.

Local and national facilities

Provision and opportunity

Fact
The provision of facilities does not automatically grant the opportunity for participation to all.

 **Key points**

- Do adequate facilities exist locally and nationally?
- Facilities are expensive to build and maintain.
- Are people able to use them?
- Even where facilities exist, they must be reachable, affordable and appropriate for the type of user.
- Some facilities will always be difficult to provide for use locally and at grass-roots level (e.g. water and mountain-based activities), as will other activities that require the use of expensive equipment and/or remote terrain.
- In order to maximise the effects that the provision of facilities has upon overall participation levels, it is necessary to consider the joint use of facilities at both local/national and grass-roots/élite levels.
- Some provision must be made for élite performers who require specialised facilities.
- Some of these facilities may also be available for use by local groups/ schools when not required for their primary purpose by élite performers.

Local provision

Facts
The major providers of local facilities are: - the local authority - private enterprise - private and voluntary clubs and associations.

 **Key points**

The local authority
- This body provides and maintains:
  - public parks
  - public playing fields
  - public swimming pools

- sports facilities in schools
- local sports centres
- local youth centres.
- Many local facilities are used jointly by schools and other community groups.
- Some local authorities also help to fund facilities such as athletics tracks, outdoor pursuits centres and water sports centres.
- Youth centres are often sited on, or adjacent to, school campuses in order to facilitate the joint use of as many facilities as possible.

Private enterprise

- An increasing range of recreational and sporting facilities are now provided by private business ventures for whom profit is a major motive.
- These tend to be private health and sports clubs offering 'executive-style' facilities for squash, tennis, fitness and health suites, and private swimming facilities.
- Such facilities are normally beyond the reach of those earning less than above average incomes.
- Many of these clubs now have several branches in different parts of the country, rather like a series of department stores, each contributing to the profit of the parent company.
- These clubs do not normally cater for large team games as the cost of acquiring and maintaining large outdoor playing areas would be unprofitable.

Private and voluntary clubs and associations

- There is a clear distinction between private clubs that are run as businesses (see above) and private non-profit-making clubs run by committees for the benefit of their members.
- Most of the officers of these clubs work on a voluntary basis.
- Some larger establishments such as golf clubs may have some full-time paid officials, but this is usually because the work-load requires full-time attention.
- These clubs are normally owned by their members or are held in trust.
- They are not owned by private investors or shareholders.
- Many of these clubs do cater for outdoor team games and some of them have considerable histories.
- Some of them make considerable efforts to enable ordinary people to join whilst others do not.

Did you know ?

That private members' sports clubs were the basis of most sport in this country. Former pupils of public schools, local churches, banks, business houses and many factory owners all provided recreational facilities, many of which are still in use today. The tennis championships at Wimbledon are run by the All England Club, who stage the event on their own (private) club premises.

focus point

Both types of private club, whether profit-making or not, are important, as they contribute to the provision of facilities for those who can afford to pay for them. This has the effect of easing the demand for facilities provided from public funding. A significant number of cricket, rugby and tennis clubs are run as private members' clubs which own their own facilities. This is in distinct contrast to soccer (and amateur rugby league in the north of England), where the majority of grass-roots clubs rent pitches on municipal recreation grounds, parks and local school playing fields.

Questions

1. Give two reasons why it will always be difficult to provide local facilities for some activities.

2. How does the joint use of sporting and recreational facilities help to increase participation levels?

3. What is the difference between a sports club run as a business and a private members' club?

4. Give examples of three different types of sporting facility normally provided and maintained by a local authority.

National provision

Fact

The provision of sporting and recreational facilities at national level is also provided through a mixture of public and private funding.

Key points

- This provision embraces a wide range of activities, from sport to public pathways, ancient buildings and sites of outstanding natural beauty.
- This is the responsibility of bodies such as:
  - the Countryside Agency
  - the Environment Agency
  - English Heritage
  - the National Trust.
- The Department of Culture, Media and Sport also has overall responsibility for:
  - museums
  - galleries and libraries
  - ancient buildings and monuments
  - the arts
  - sport
  - education
  - broadcasting and the media
  - tourism
  - the creative industries
  - the National Lottery.
- National Lottery funding that is earmarked for sports projects is channelled through the Department of Culture, Media and Sport and the appropriate Sports Councils in England, Northern Ireland, Scotland and Wales, or through UK Sport.
- This is slowly changing and the recent restructuring of sports councils, together with the availability of National Lottery funding, is slowly helping to change old attitudes.
- UK Sport now concerns itself with Great Britain matters, while the sports councils of the four home countries administer sport within each of their own areas.
- Other countries have for some time been developing facilities for sport using public funding:
  - in Australia, major facilities are developed using a combination of state funding and private sponsorship
  - in France, the stadium for the 1998 World Cup Competition was entirely funded by the state
  - in other European countries, many of the major football stadia are municipally owned and rented to clubs for major league and cup games.

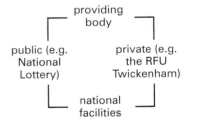

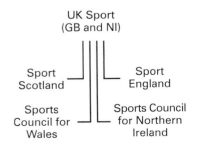

focus point

In the UK we have a legacy of privately owned stadia as major sporting venues, the most obvious examples being in association football and county cricket. Only recently, with developments such as the National Stadium in Cardiff and the National Cycling Centre in Manchester, have we begun to develop facilities which are built, at least partly, by central funding. This legacy is partly due to the tradition of clubs owning their own grounds, but it also reflects the traditional resistance in this country to government involvement in sport.

UK Sport
|
Sport England
|
sports national governing bodies
|
national centres of excellence
|
regional centres of excellence
|
clubs, athletes and coaches

National centres of excellence

Fact

The five national sports centres (see below) were originally intended to be the only centres of excellence.

Key points

- Following the review of sports councils and the creation of the United Kingdom Institute of Sport, this structure now includes national and regional centres of excellence.
- Existing national sports centres may house some national centres of excellence, whilst other sports may be based at other venues with excellent facilities.
- A centre of excellence may have national or regional status, but in some case it may have both, e.g. Lilleshall is the national centre of excellence for gymnastics and also serves as the West Midlands regional centre.
- Some national centres of excellence (e.g. swimming at the University of Bath) are not national sports centres but have very good facilities for a particular sport.
- Another example of this is the national centre of excellence for cycling at Sports City in Manchester.
- National Sports Centres are situated at:
  - Crystal Palace (south-east London)
  - Bisham Abbey (Buckinghamshire)
  - Holme Pierrepont (Nottinghamshire).
  - Lilleshall (Shropshire)
  - Plas y Brenin (North Wales)

Sports institutes

Fact

The increasingly common trend to create sports institutes grew out of the success of Soviet and Eastern bloc athletes of the 1960s, 1970s and 1980s.

Key points

- Sports institutes work on the principle of housing specialist facilities, coaching, medical support and organisational infrastructure in a small number of well-equipped, well-funded centres.
- France adopted this structure after Olympic failure in Rome in 1960.
- Australia did likewise following poor results in Montreal in 1976.
- The UK Institute of Sport was set up following poor performances in Atlanta in 1996.
- The current structure in the UK is administered by UK Sport, which is the senior sports authority in the UK following the restructuring of the former Sports Council in 1997.

- The sports council for each of the four 'home' countries will look after its own sports institute in matters which are not UK- or GB-related.
- The English Institute of Sport has a network of regional centres.
- Northern Ireland, Scotland and Wales are developing their own structures centred at Ulster, Stirling and Cardiff respectively.
- The network centres of each of the four home countries will make up the United Kingdom Sports Institute (UKSI).
- The regional centres in England are:
  - North West (Manchester)
  - Yorkshire (Sheffield)
  - East (University of East Anglia)
  - East Midlands (Holme Pierrepont)
  - West Midlands (Lilleshall)
  - South East (Crystal Palace)
  - South (Bisham Abbey)
  - South West (Bath University)
  - North (Gateshead)
  - South Coast (Southampton).
- The current Sport England slogan is 'More medals, more people, more places'.
- While medals are important, it is also essential to have as many active participants as possible.
- Sporting success is more likely if the top performers are chosen from a wide selection base.
- Funding must therefore be targeted at grass-roots level as well as élite sports groups.
- This not only helps win gold medals, but creates a healthier nation.

UK Sports Institute

	UK Sports Institute	
English network centres	—	English Institute of Sport
Northern Ireland network centres	–	Northern Ireland Institute of Sport
Scottish network centres	—	Scottish Institute of Sport
Welsh network centres	–	Welsh Institute of Sport

Did you know

That Germany set up sports institutes in the years leading up to the Olympics in Berlin in 1936.

Questions

1. Why do we need to have an overall authority for British sport as well as sports councils for each of the four 'home' countries?

2. Why are some centres of excellence not based at national sports centres?

3. Give two reasons why it is important to make provision for grass-roots participation as well as for éite sports performers.

4. Name a major sporting facility made possible by National Lottery funding.

Exam tips

You need to understand:

- how sports facilities and opportunities both nationally and locally affect participation in physical activities
- what sporting facilities are available in your locality (and be able to give examples)
- what is meant by the following terms: local authority provision, private enterprise, voluntary organisations, and national authorities (and be able to give examples)
- the role of national centres of excellence in promoting and supporting the development of sporting excellence.

Key Words

provision
opportunity
participation
municipal
grass-roots
local provision
private enterprise
voluntary clubs
private members' clubs
public funding
national provision
centre of excellence
Institute of Sport

Components of fitness

What is fitness?

fitness components

- cardiovascular
- endurance
- muscular endurance
- speed
- strength
- flexibility

Facts

There is no one single aspect of human performance that constitutes fitness. Different activities and lifestyles may require very different programmes of preparation or training. Question: 'Are you fit'? Response: 'Fit for what?'

 **Key points**

Cardiovascular endurance

- This is the capacity of the heart and circulatory system to meet the demands of sustained activity.
- It develops as a result of long-term training and produces an increase in the size of the heart muscles (cardiac hypertrophy).
- It is this increase in size that allows the heart to pump a greater volume of blood around the body.
- Cardiac output in a trained endurance athlete can rise to seven or eight times its normal level.
- Some people are born with this advantage but it can be improved with regular training.
- An efficient cardiovascular system benefits everyone, as the heart does not have to work as hard to pump blood around the body.

Muscular endurance

- This is the capacity of the muscles to perform contractions at near-maximum level for an extended period.
- This is very important in events where power must be applied for a sustained period.
- Muscles depend upon the body's lactic acid system being efficient enough to keep accumulation levels below that at which the muscles become fatigued.

Speed

- This is not just about how fast a person can run.
- In many sports, the speed with which other movements can be performed is also important.
- Many authorities consider speed to be an innate ability, but it can be improved with training.
- It can also be improved simply by moving more efficiently (correct technique).

Strength

- Strength is 'the maximum force that can be developed within a muscle or group of muscles during a single maximal contraction'.
- The above refers to a very specific single all-out effort.

- There are other types of strength which involve repeated efforts, such as those required of the rugby forward in scrimmaging.
- Refers to a movement or movements that require some effort.
- Most individuals require a degree of strength for many activities, sporting or otherwise.
- Unless such activities occur regularly, we may not be capable of performing them when required to.

Flexibility

- Flexibility is determined by several factors, including the elasticity of ligaments, tendons and muscle attachments.
- It may be defined as 'the range of movement possible at a single joint or at a number of joints'.
- The same degree of flexibility is not achieved at all joints because of their different construction.
- All individuals require some degree of flexibility, which should be part of any training programme.
- Some activities demand a level of flexibility that requires years of specialised preparation.
- The ability to bend, stretch and twist allows us to perform normal daily activities.
- Inactivity is the greatest cause of loss of flexibility.

Skill-related fitness

Facts

Whilst physiological aspects of fitness are important, the ability to perform skilful movements also requires specific qualities. Many of these are innate but can be improved with training. Skill-related components include:

- agility
- balance
- co-ordination.
- speed of reaction
- timing

skill-related components

- agility
- balance
- co-ordination
- speed of reaction
- timing

Key points

Agility

- This is the ability to move in a controlled way and to turn, stop and start quickly.
- Agility is sometimes confused with flexibility.
- Agility is to do with the control/adjustment of the body, rather than its flexibility.

Balance

- This is an important aspect of any physical activity or movement.
- Balance is the control of our centre of mass in relation to our base of support.
- It is as important in doing everyday things as it is in sport and recreation.

Co-ordination

- This is the result of interaction between the body's motor (movement) system and the nervous system.
- It enables various parts of the body to produce a desired movement or sequence of movements.
- It is essential for the successful execution of many sporting skills.
- It is an innate ability, possessed to a greater degree by some individuals than by others.
- Co-ordination can be improved with practice that is focused on specific skills or activities.

Speed of reaction

- Reaction time – the time between the initial stimulus and the initiation of a response.
- Movement time – the time between the initiation of a response and the completion of the resultant movement.
- Response time – the total amount of time between from the initial stimulus, a response, and the completion of that response.

Timing

- Timing is not always to do with speed.
- It concerns the execution of a movement at the appropriate time and in the most effective way (e.g. the timing of a pass in rugby or soccer).
- It can be influenced by other skill-related components and a perception of what is going on around us (e.g. opponents, movement of the ball or a gusting wind).

reaction time
+
movement time
=
response time

focus point

Co-ordination, speed of reaction and timing are inter-related in that all three aspects are often crucial in the performance of complex skills. In terms of training and/or practice, it is often event-specific activities that are the most appropriate means of improvement – where all three skill-related components can often be addressed simultaneously.

Questions

1. Why does cardiac hypertrophy make it easier for the heart to pump blood around the body?

2. What is the difference between muscular strength and muscular endurance?

3. Why is it that a greater range of movement is obtainable at some joints than others?

4. How would you explain the difference between 'agility' and 'balance'?

5. Similarly, how would you differentiate between 'co-ordination' and 'timing'?

Key Words

cardiovascular endurance
muscular endurance
flexibility
cardiac hypertrophy
innate
maximal contraction
agility
balance
co-ordination
reaction
timing

Exam tips

You need to understand:

- How preparation, training and fitness relate to and affect performance.
- The different components of health-related fitness: cardiovascular endurance, muscular endurance, speed, strength and flexibility.
- The different components of skill-related fitness: agility, balance, co-ordination, speed of reaction and timing.
- How the above components of fitness relate to good health and affect performance in a variety of physical activities.

Factors affecting fitness

A healthy diet

Facts

Although training and exercise are important, there are other factors that also contribute to fitness and good health. We need food for three reasons:

- growth
- energy
- tissue replacement and repair.

 **points**

factors affecting fitness

- diet
- physical differences
- age, gender and disability
- minimising the difference/ slowing down the decline
- lifestyle influences

Carbohydrates

- Carbohydrates are high in glucose (energy) and are stored in the liver and kidneys.
- They are the most readily available form of energy.
- Energy can be stored in the form of carbohydrate.
- They are important for endurance athletes, who need large stores of energy.
- Eating large amounts of carbohydrate-rich food is often referred to as carbo-loading.

Protein

- Protein supplies approximately 10 per cent of daily energy requirements.
- It also assists in tissue growth and blood haemoglobin levels.
- Protein should be approximately one-sixth of the daily calorific intake.
- It is found in red meat, dairy products, fish, poultry, beans and pulses.

Fats

- Fats supply around 70 per cent of our energy requirements.
- Fat is the body's preferred energy source (other than intensive bursts).
- Excessive fat is stored in the body tissues and causes obesity.
- No more than one-third of our daily nutritional needs should be in the form of fat.

Minerals

- Minerals are required by the body for building tissue.
- The most common ones are:
  - calcium – forms bones and teeth
  - sodium – regulates body fluids
  - iron – helps in the transport of oxygen by red blood cells
  - iodine – used in hormone formation.

Vitamins

- Vitamins occur in two main groups:
  - fat soluble vitamins – vitamins A, D, E and K
  - water soluble vitamins – vitamins B and C.

Food group	Required intake
Carbohydrate	60%
Protein	15%
Fats	20%
Minerals	Minute quantities
Vitamins	A, B complex, C, D, E and K
Fibre	30g per day
Water	5 litres (approx)

Did you know

That it is dangerous to take vitamin supplements in excess of the recommended daily requirements.

- They help in the following ways. They:
  - aid growth
  - increase resistance to infection
  - regulate certain of the body's functions
  - help the metabolism of certain foods and help to avoid deficiencies.

Fibre

- Fibre regulates the digestive system.
- It helps to retain water.
- It is an important component in the removal of waste products.

Water

- Water helps to remove unabsorbed food and other waste products.
- It is essential for the body's chemical reactions.
- Water assists in turning stored fat into energy.
- Water reduces sodium build-up in the body.
- It helps to maintain muscle tone.
- It helps rid the body of waste and toxins.

Did you know

That our bodies are more than 70 per cent water.

Physical differences

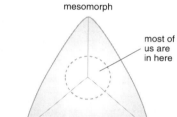

The three body types are like the points in a triangle

Facts

The human race embraces a range of physical characteristics. For certain sports, a particular body type is advantageous, but many cater for a wide range of physical attributes. The three main body types are classified as:

- ectomorph
- endomorph
- mesomorph.

Key points

Ectomorph

- An ectomorph is very slightly built, possessing narrow shoulders and hips and often long limbs.
- They are often referred to as 'skinny' or 'scrawny'.

Endomorph

- An endomorph typically possesses a round or 'pear-drop' shape with narrow shoulders but broad hips.
- They often carry excess weight around the waist, hips and upper thighs.

Mesomorph

- A mesomorph is a typical 'athletic build' with broad shoulders, narrow hips and well-developed chest.
- They are often typified as an 'inverted triangle' – the exact opposite of the endomorph.

Height and weight

- Height and weight are particularly significant in some sporting activities.

- Tall people will have a distinct advantage in some activities but not in others.
- Mobility and speed may well be adversely affected by those who are bulky and/or overweight.
- Size advantage is minimised in sports where there are weight classes, as in wrestling and boxing.
- Fat should represent no more than 20 per cent of bodyweight for men and 30 per cent for women.

Age, gender and disability

Facts

- Age, gender and disability each have an influence on attainable and maintainable levels of fitness.
- We cannot prevent ageing or ignore differences between the sexes, but we can take action to help minimise them.
- Disability should never be interpreted as inability.

 **points**

Age

- Our bodies slow down with age.
- Continued physical activity is clearly beneficial, with some sensible limitations.
- Muscular strength declines with age, but endurance levels can be maintained with regular activity.
- Bones become brittle and the capacity to withstand impact injuries declines.
- Reaction and limb speed decline, but this can be delayed through continued activity.
- Numbers of older people involved in sport and recreation is growing rapidly.
- The physiological components of fitness and skill are all affected by age.
- This decline (or ageing process) can be slowed down by continued participation in physical activities.

Gender

- Generally, females are not as physically strong as males and may not compete on an equal basis.
- Women often perform better than men in endurance events.
- Women have a 30 per cent greater fat content than men and this may contribute to their ability to endure physical hardship.
- Changing attitudes to 'appropriate activities' for women will allow female performances in previously 'all-male' sports to improve rapidly.

Disability

- Gender limitations and the effects of ageing still apply.
- Social prejudices have changed markedly.

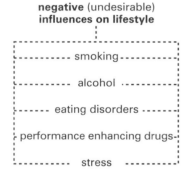

For disability performers, fitness principles still apply but with some modification

- Technology now allows participation for those who were previously excluded.
- Disability sport is now becoming mainstream.
- Disability performers are limited only by their determination, just as in all other sporting activity.
- Disability athletes can produce remarkable physical performances if given the opportunity to do so.
- Disability participants will have some limitations but will still benefit as they get older.

Questions

1. Name the three energy-giving food groups.

2. There are two main groups of vitamins. How would you identify them?

3. In which aspect of physical performance do women equal and sometimes out-perform men?

Lifestyle influences

negative (undesirable) **influences on lifestyle**

- smoking
- alcohol
- eating disorders
- performance enhancing drugs
- stress

Facts

The most direct agents of influence on our lifestyle are our parents, friends, other adults (such as teachers) and role models in sport, popular music and the media. All the negative influences listed below may:
- be injurious to our general health
- have a detrimental influence on sporting performance or contribute to cheating.

Key points

Smoking

- At one time socially acceptable but no longer so.
- We are now much more informed about the harmful effects of tobacco.
- Although recent figures show a decline, there are still 450 young people who take up smoking every day in the UK.
- Smoking affects fitness in the following ways:
  - it increases the likelihood of heart malfunction
  - it increases the likelihood of thrombosis
  - it damages and reduces the capacity and efficiency of the lungs
  - it reduces the oxygen-carrying capacity of the blood
  - it limits the efficiency of gaseous exchange.

Alcohol

- Alcohol consumption is considered to be far more socially acceptable than smoking but it can still be harmful to health if consumed excessively.
- For sports performers, alcohol can:

Did you know ?

That smoking kills 120,000 people every year in the United Kingdom.

- artificially steady the nerves prior to and during performance
- delay or mask feelings of tiredness/exhaustion.
- Unwanted side-effects of alcohol consumption:
  - dehydration
  - slower heart rate, creating an unfair advantage
  - possible liver damage
  - slower reaction time and/or false assessment of risky situations.

Eating disorders

- The term 'eating disorder' is an illness rather than the result of poor diet.
- As with many other lifestyle problems, eating disorders are damaging on two levels:
  - they affect general health and well-being
  - they affect active sportspeople who have great emphasis placed on their body shape.
- The most common types of eating disorder are:
  - anorexia nervosa – self-imposed starvation, with sufferers obsessed with 'being fat'
  - bulimia nervosa – sufferers have a poor self-image; binge eating is usually followed by vomiting and feelings of self-disgust.
- Anorexia nervosa and bulimia nervosa affect more women than men.
- The emphasis on body shape/size in some sports is often used to justify excessive 'thinness'.
- The highest incidence seems to be associated with sports such as gymnastics, distance running, horse racing, figure skating, dancing and bodybuilding.
- Compulsive eating disorder usually takes the form of uncontrolled episodes of secretive over-eating.
- Compulsive eating disorder is not usually related to athletic performance or exercise obsession.

Performance enhancing drugs

- Performance enhancing drugs are taken, usually knowingly, with the intention of gaining unfair advantage over one's opponents.
- Stimulants:
  - The most common stimulants are amphetamines, which mask the effects of tiredness and increase feelings of aggression.
  - They are normally associated with endurance events such as cycling and long distance swimming.
- Narcotic analgesics:
  - These are effectively painkillers, often used by sports performers to mask the pain of injury.
- Anabolic steroids:
  - These are artificial substances that reproduce those which occur in the body naturally (e.g. testosterone).
  - They are most commonly used in the building of muscle bulk and accelerating recovery from intense training.
  - They also produce dangerous long-term side effects, which are very injurious to health.
- Diuretics:
  - Diuretics have the effect of expelling water from the body faster than is normally the case.

- They are commonly used in horse racing and in other sports where bodyweight is critically important.
- They are also sometimes taken to mask the presence of other substances.
- Erythropoietin:
    - This is more usually referred to as EPO.
    - It is largely undetectable after 72 hours.
    - It greatly increases the production of red blood cells, which carry oxygen to the muscles.
    - It is of significant benefit in endurance events.
- Blood doping:
    - This involves the removal and later replacement of blood to increase its oxygen-carrying capacity.
    - Blood doping can produce a 20 per cent increase in blood haemoglobin levels.

Stress

- Moderate levels can produce improvements in performance.
- Extreme levels can demotivate and seriously depress performance levels.
- The latter instance is normally referred to as over-arousal.
- Stress levels can be managed in any of the following ways:
    - setting attainable targets
    - mental rehearsal and positive imagery
    - verbal reassurance from coach and/or supporters
    - relaxation, both physical and mental.
- The same stimulus, e.g. a noisy crowd, can act as a positive influence on one performer whilst it might be seriously demotivating for another.
- Similarly, the 'big occasion' will bring out the best in some players but may be totally overwhelming for others.

Questions

1. What is meant by the term 'balanced diet'?

2. Name two sports with which each of the 'classic' body types are often associated.

3. Give two examples of how physical capability declines with age.

4. Why is alcohol a banned substance for sports performers?

5. Explain the difference between an eating disorder and poor diet.

Key Words

carbohydrates protein
fats minerals
vitamins fibre
water ectomorph
endomorph mesomorph
gender disability
ageing lifestyle
thrombosis anorexia
bulimia nervosa
  nervosa compulsive
narcotic eating
  analgesics disorder
anabolic diuretics
  steroids stress
erythropoietin
  (EPO)

Exam tips

You need to understand:

- what is meant by good health and fitness and the factors that affect this
- the role a healthy diet plays in good health and fitness
- how differences in physique, including height and weight, can affect success in different activities
- The effects that smoking, excessive alcohol, over-eating and under-eating, performance enhancing drugs and stress can have on performance, health and well-being.

Investigation of the effect of fitness on performance and how to assess it

Testing and measurement

Facts

Fitness and skill tests are not intended to improve fitness but to monitor it. The OCR specification requires you to be familiar with seven such tests, which are shown in the diagram here.

 **points**

The multistage fitness test

- This test is also known as the bleep test.
- It is a convenient means of testing large groups of people.
- The test provides a reasonably accurate estimate of VO_2 max.
- VO_2 max is the maximum amount of oxygen (in millilitres) that we are able to use in one minute for every kilogram of our bodyweight.
- The test has 21 levels, each of which lasts for one minute.
- It is performed by running up and down a 20-metre course.
- Runs must be timed to coincide with the 'beep' at each end of the course.
- The number of shuttles and the running speed increase at each level.
- Very appropriate for games players but perhaps not ideal for those whose events require continuous steady activity.
- At the end of the test, the VO_2 max score is obtained from the test tables.

The 12-minute run

- This test is a good indicator of endurance and also provides an approximate VO_2 max score.
- The distance can be marked out on any suitable flat surface.
- Markers are placed at 100-metre intervals.
- The aim is to run as many 400-metre circuits plus 100-metre intervals as possible within 12 minutes.
- The total distance for the 12-minute period is calculated by adding the number of 400-metre circuits to the number of 100-metre intervals covered during the final lap.
- The test supplies tables calibrated by age group and has separate ones for younger and older athletes.

Sprint tests

- Sprints can be used either to test/monitor performance or as part of a programme of training.
- They can also be used to predict performance potential and to measure velocity, acceleration and maximum speed.

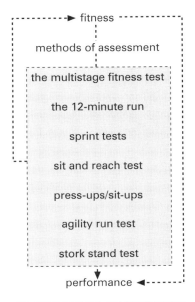

fitness
methods of assessment
the multistage fitness test
the 12-minute run
sprint tests
sit and reach test
press-ups/sit-ups
agility run test
stork stand test
performance

focus point

It is important that this test should not become a 'competition' between those taking part. Participants are encouraged to continue until they can run no further and there are inherent dangers in this. BAALPE advises that students with respiratory, heart or other associated problems should not take part.

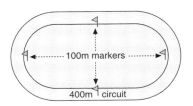

100m markers

400m circuit

A 12-minute run course

Did you know ❓

That shot putters use sprint training as part of their preparation.

- These tests are useful for games players as well as sprinters.
- The most common sprint tests are:
  - 30-metre acceleration test – monitors acceleration from a standing (or block) start and can be used to predict times for longer sprints
  - 60-metre sprint test – measures sustained speed
  - 30-metre flying sprint test – performed and timed as a 'flying' section of a longer sprint
  - the Running-based Anaerobic Sprint Test (RAST test) – the most sophisticated test, measuring power output and fatigue levels.

Sit and reach test

- The sit and reach test is a test of flexibility for the hip, hamstrings and lower back muscles.
- The legs must be fully extended and the soles of the feet flat against the test apparatus.
- Measurement is of the distance reached by the fingertips past the line of the toes.
- The better of two attempts is the one recorded.
- It should be remembered that flexibility is important for participants in all activities, whether or not it is identified as a specific component of fitness.

The sit and reach test

Press-ups/sit-ups

- These exercises are good general indicators of muscular endurance in:
  - the arms and shoulders (press-ups)
  - the abdominal region (sit-ups).
- Both of these activities should be modified for older or younger performers.
- It is also dangerous for individuals who are considerably overweight to attempt full press-ups; modified press-ups using the knees as pivot points or gym benches to 'raise the floor' can minimise this risk.
- Sit-ups should be performed with bent knees to reduce the risk of abdominal or internal injury (bent-knee sit-ups).
- Both of these activities can be used as part of a specific or general exercise programme in addition to being useful measurements of progress; when used in the former way they should of course be part of a whole exercise regime and not simply repeated in isolation.

Agility run test

- This test is also known as the Illinois Agility Run.
- It is an excellent test of agility, balance and speed.
- It is an excellent test of potential for team and racquet games players.
- It is not a good test of stamina or endurance.
- The test is an indicator of potential or a test of progress – it is not a method of training.

A course for the agility run test

Stork stand test

- This is a test of balance.
- It is sometimes also referred to as the blind stork test, when the subject is blindfolded.
- As in other tests, repeated practice of the test itself may improve your score but this will not necessarily produce any improvement in balance in other situations.

Questions

1. Why is the agility run test a more useful indication of potential good games players than the multistage fitness test?

2. Why is a 30-metre flying sprint test a better indication of potential maximum sprinting speed than a 30-metre sprint from a standing start?

Exam tips

You need to understand:

- how training principles and methods can be used to enhance performance
- how testing and measuring can be used to evaluate an individual's suitability for an activity and identify potential strengths and weaknesses
- the multistage fitness test and the 12-minute run as tests of cardiovascular fitness
- at least one test to measure each of the following: sprinting speed, flexibility, muscular endurance, agility and balance.

focus point

The point about repeated practice is worth serious thought. In any of the tests in this section, performance in these tests will of course improve if you practice them often enough. This, however, defeats the object of the tests. They are intended to indicate either your natural level of ability or the degree to which that ability has improved as a result of other skill or fitness training activities. They are tests of fitness or skill, not methods of training.

Key Words

bleep test
VO_2 max
shuttle
acceleration
sustained speed
30-metre flying sprint test
RAST test
modified press-ups
bent-knee sit-ups
potential
blind stork test

Fitness training principles

Planning and monitoring a personal exercise programme

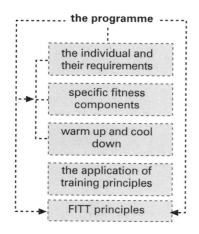

the programme
- the individual and their requirements
- specific fitness components
- warm up and cool down
- the application of training principles
- FITT principles

Fact

A personal exercise programme should be just that – personal!

 **Key points**

The individual and their requirements
- Why does the individual wish to exercise/train?
- Is the individual young or old, male or female?
- Is the individual a novice or an experienced participant?
- Is the programme for general health?
- Is the programme for a specific activity?

Specific fitness components
- All fitness components should be addressed with an emphasis that reflects the particular needs of the individual.
- An activity-specific programme should also stress activity-specific components.
- In a general exercise program all components may not be accommodated in the same session (see table).
- Fitness- and skill-related components can be mixed for variety but isolated for specialist sessions.
- There should be at least three sessions per week.
- This would be insufficient for élite performers.
- Emphasis on particular fitness components may be changed according to the time of the year and the stage of the training programme.

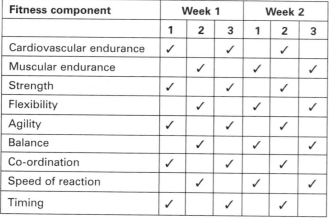

Fitness component	Week 1			Week 2		
	1	2	3	1	2	3
Cardiovascular endurance	✓		✓		✓	
Muscular endurance		✓		✓		✓
Strength	✓		✓		✓	
Flexibility		✓		✓		✓
Agility	✓		✓		✓	
Balance		✓		✓		✓
Co-ordination	✓		✓		✓	
Speed of reaction		✓		✓		✓
Timing	✓		✓		✓	

Warm up and cool down
- The warm up:
  - The body should be gradually prepared for physical exercise.
  - The pulse rate should be gradually raised to a level approaching that of the activity.
  - Joint flexibility should be addressed with moderate stretching and mobility exercises.
  - The skills or movements used should be event-specific.
  - The routine should also include mental preparation/focusing.
  - The warm up environment should at least approximate that of competition.

- The cool down:
  - The body's systems must be allowed to return gradually to their normal resting state.
  - It is also inadvisable to suddenly stop all activity.
  - Heart rate should be lowered gradually in order to avoid blood pooling in the muscles.
  - The cool down also promotes removal of waste products and the dissipation of lactic acid build-up.

The application of training principles

Fact

It is essential to understand the principles that govern the acquisition, maintenance and loss of fitness.

training principles

- overload
- specificity
- progression
- peaking
- reversibility

points

Overload

- We can only make improvements in physical performance by forcing the body to work beyond its current limits.
- This applies to strength, endurance and physical mobility.
- Workloads must be increased gradually as training progresses.
- The body responds by adapting to this increasing workload.
- Overload should not exceed 5 to 10 per cent of existing capability.
- The rate at which the body adapts will vary according to the experience of the performer.
- A beginner will make much more rapid advances.
- Targets should be increased as the body adapts and progression is achieved.

Overload can be achieved by:

- increasing the resistance
- increasing the number of repetitions
- increasing the number of sets
- increasing the frequency of sessions
- increasing the intensity of sessions
- *reducing* the rest periods between sessions.

Specificity

- Training should be specific to the intended activity.
- Specificity training should also recognise that different sports utilise different energy systems.
- A 5000-metre runner relies on aerobic energy.
- A games player utilises both energy systems.
- A weightlifter utilises only anaerobic energy.

specificity and energy system use		
5000 metres	aerobic	
games player		
weightlifter	anaerobic	

Progression

- All training programmes should promote progression.
- The intention should be to move from general aims to specific targets at specified times.
- Targets should be agreed by performer and coach.
- Progression can be achieved by ensuring that three specific pathways are followed:
  - easy to difficult (overload/adaptability)

progression in exercise and training

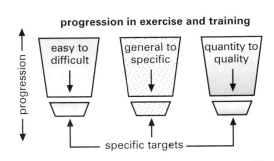

progression

easy to difficult

general to specific

quantity to quality

specific targets

- general to specific (specificity)
- quantity to quality (peaking).

Peaking

- Athletes can only operate at their absolute best for a limited period of time.
- In some sports it is vitally important to peak for a specific event or competition.
- Training programmes are broken down into phases or periods, known as periodisation.

Reversibility

- Reversibility dictates the rate at which fitness is lost during any periods of inactivity (e.g. injury or illness).
- Fitness levels can decline at the rate of one-third of the time they took to gain.
- A beginner will lose fitness far more quickly than an experienced performer.
- Fitness in some components should not be gained at the expense of others.

FITT principles

> ### Fact
>
> FITT principles suggest that all training programmes should include the following:
> - **F**requency of training or exercise
> - **I**ntensity of training or exercise
> - **T**ime of training or exercise
> - **T**ype of training or exercise.

 **Key points**

Frequency

- The frequency of training sessions should reflect the needs of the individual and/or specific activity.
- Three sessions per week is the minimum needed to maintain healthy fitness levels.
- It is not uncommon for some top-level performers to train two or even three times a day.

Intensity

- Intensity of training is governed by the purpose/level of the programme.
- For improvement in fitness the heart rate must be raised to between 60 and 85 per cent of the maximum heart rate (MHR); this is known as the safe training zone.

Time

- 30 minutes of brisk activity should raise the heart rate above the 60 per cent of the MHR threshold.

- This can be increased as progress permits and the nature of a particular activity demands.

Type

- The type of activity should reflect the specific needs of the individual or group concerned.
- The type of activity should also reflect the period of training.

Questions

1. Why is it important to consider the individual when designing a fitness programme?

2. Why do élite performers place particular emphasis on some specific training components?

3. How would you ensure that progression is built in to a weight-training programme?

Exam tips

You need to understand:

- the benefits of regular, safe exercise in relation to personal fitness and health
- how to use training principles to plan, implement and monitor a six-week personal exercise programme for the purpose of a) general health and well-being, or b) a specific activity
- how training principles can be applied to a training programme to improve performance
- how FITT principles can be applied to training programmes for specific activities.

Key Words

specific fitness components
event-specific
overload
specificity
peaking
periodisation
MHR

skill-related components
blood pooling
progression
reversibility
FITT
safe training zone

Training methods

Training for specific activities

```
                    training
          ┌────────────┴────────────┐
      specific                   general
     preparation                  health
          └──────── training ──────┘
                   principles
                       │
              training methods
     ┌──────────┬──────┴──────┬──────────┐
  circuit     fartlek       interval
  training                  training
     ┌──────────┬─────────────┬──────────┐
 continuous   flexibility    weight
  training      training     training
```

Facts
- Training can serve two functions:
  - activity to promote all-round health and fitness
  - as preparation for a specific purpose.
- Training methods apply to general or specialised training.

Key points

Circuit training
- This method of training consists of a series of exercises.
- Circuits can be designed to develop all components of training and for novices or experts.
- A circuit normally has between six and ten workstations, each of which exercises a particular muscle group.
- Each circuit is completed and a short rest is taken before further circuits are undertaken.
- Progression is based on the number of circuits, the number of exercises performed, or the reduction of the rest period between each circuit.
- Targets based on time taken or the number of repetitions can be set for each exercise or circuit.
- The number of repetitions is normally based on half of the maximum repetitions an athlete can perform.
- After several sessions, targets can be reset to reflect any improvements that have been made.
- Useful for games players who need to develop both fitness and skill components.

Continuous training
- Continuous training is also known as steady state training.
- If work rate is too high, the body runs out of oxygen.
- If work rate is too low, there is no training benefit.
- A major benefit is improved endurance (aerobic capacity).
- Aerobics, cycling, dancing, running and swimming are the most common types of continuous training.

Fartlek
- Fartlek is a Swedish word meaning 'speed play'.
- Steady-paced running is interspersed with almost flat-out bursts of speed.
- The steady-paced (aerobic) running acts as recovery from the flat-out (anaerobic) bursts.
- This form of training therefore develops both aerobic and anaerobic fitness.
- Applications include distance runners and road cyclists who need to change pace to make or respond to attacks, and games players who use frequent short bursts of flat-out activity.

Did you know

That steady state training is very beneficial for older performers or others who have been inactive for some time.

Flexibility training

- Joints should be stretched to a point just beyond their limit and held for around ten seconds.
- Movements should not be performed violently or beyond the point of marginal discomfort.
- Active stretching – some joints can be mobilised easily without any assistance.
- Passive stretching – a full range of movement sometimes needs partner assistance; the performer is passive, with the partner gently stretching.
- Stretching and/or flexibility exercises should:
  - occur as part of the training programme
  - address all the major joints, especially those that come under particular stress during an event
  - take place three times a week
  - also be part of warm up and cool down routines.
- A hurdler might perform the exercises illustrated here as part of a warm up.

Stretching the hamstrings and adductor muscles

Interval training

- Interval training means exactly what it says: training with short intervals or recovery periods.
- A specialised form of training, with specified periods of activity followed by recovery periods.
- Progression is achieved by adjusting the repetitions and the periods of recovery.
- The number of sets can be adjusted to training needs.
- This method is very effective for performers whose events cover a precise distance.
- Interval training accommodates both under or over-distance work and the setting of precise targets.
- Distances can be broken down into smaller units, each one being completed at faster than race pace.

focus point

You should be aware of specific stretching exercises that apply to any sports in which you participate. You should also know at least one stretching exercise for each of the major joints.

Interval training for an 800-metre runner

Personal best = 2 min.

Target time = 1 min. 50 sec.

Phase 1:

Schedule	
	6 × 200m in 29 sec. : 3 min. rest
	6 × 200m in 29 sec. : 2 min. rest
	6 × 200m in 29 sec. : 1 min. rest
	3 × 400m in 58 sec. : 3 min. rest
	3 × 400m in 58 sec. : 2 min. rest
	3 × 400m in 58 sec. : 1 min. rest

Time trial 800m = 1 min. 56 sec.

Phase 2 (re-set times and intervals):

Schedule	
	6 × 200m in 27 sec. : 3 min. rest, etc.
	3 × 400m in 56 sec. : 3 min. rest, etc.

> ## Questions
>
> 1. How would the activities in a general exercise circuit differ from a circuit designed for a rugby forward?
>
> 2. Why is circuit training particularly suited to the needs of games players?
>
> 3. What are the similarities between interval training and circuit training?

Weight training (isometric and isotonic)

- Weightlifting is a sport; weight training is a method of training.
- Such activity should not be undertaken without expert advice or qualified supervision.
- Weight training is a very adaptable method of improving several components of fitness, although it is most commonly (and misleadingly) associated with building big muscles.
- Traditionally exercises are performed using free weights.
- Modern weight training machines permit a wider range of exercise and far safer exercises.
- Weight training can be part of a general fitness programme or it can be used to develop specific fitness components.
- Weight training utilises the principle of progression by allowing a gradual increase in the amount of weight used; this is often referred to as progressive resistance training.
- The number of repetitions performed and the recovery period between each set of repetitions can be adjusted to suit the requirements of individual training programmes.
- Weight training is most typically used to develop muscular strength and muscular endurance.
- Muscular strength:
    - All work should be at or near maximum capability.
    - The number of repetitions in each set should be six or less.
    - Weights used should be at least 85 per cent of the maximum for any given exercise in order for gains in muscular strength to be achieved.
    - Maximums for each exercise should be re-tested periodically to take account of improvement in strength levels.
    - Free weights should not be used other than with supervision.
- Muscular endurance:
    - Improvements in muscular endurance are achieved by using weights at around 50 to 60 per cent of maximum capacity in any given exercise.
    - The number of repetitions should be between 20 and 30.
    - Pyramid sets should not be employed as there would be no benefit.
    - Some weight training should continue during the season to ensure that any strength gains are not lost during the competitive period.
    - A light weight can permit full range of movement at a particular joint without the use of a partner.
- Care should be exercised in weight selection and the manner in which the exercises are performed.
- Free weight exercises can also be used in circuit training, provided that low weights are used or support is available.

- A criticism of weight training is that it does not develop all-round (i.e. aerobic) fitness.
- By combining weights with other activities, both muscular and aerobic endurance can be addressed.
- Isometric contractions:
  - This involves the contraction of a muscle against an immovable resistance.
  - It can be achieved by using weights well beyond the performer's capability.
  - It only improves muscle strength in one static position.
- Isotonic contractions:
  - This involves the contraction of a muscle throughout a range of movement.
  - It improves strength (or endurance) throughout the movement range.

Did you know ?

That if repetitions are less than 20 there is no gain in muscular endurance.

A thrower with a maximum squat of 200kg wishing to develop upper leg strength might undertake:

Session A:
3 sets of 6 repetitions, each set performed with 170kg on the leg press machine
Alternated with:

Session B (pyramid sets):
- 1 set of 5 repetitions with 170kg
- 1 set of 3 repetitions with 185kg
- 1 set of 1 repetition with 200kg (max).

A triple-jumper, who needs muscular strength and endurance, could develop both in different sessions:
- 3 sets of 30 repetitions with 100kg on the squat machine, leading to 3 sets of 30 repetitions with 120kg (endurance)
- pyramid sets of:
  - 5 × 160kg
  - 3 × 180kg
  - 1 × 200kg (strength).

Questions

1. Give one advantage of modern weight training machines over traditional free weights.

2. What is the difference between muscular strength and muscular endurance?

3. What is meant by the term 'pyramid set' in weight training?

Exam tips

You need to understand:

- how different training methods can be used to prepare for specific activities and general exercise
- the following training methods and be able to describe how to use them: circuit training, continuous training, fartlek, flexibility training, interval training, weight training
- methods of displaying data from different training methods and how to interpret such information
- the advantages and disadvantages of the above training methods.

Key Words

circuit	workstations
progression	repetitions
fitness and	steady state
skill	training
components	fartlek
recovery	sets
recovery	free weights
progressive	pyramid sets
resistance	isometric
training	isotonic

Training effects

Immediate short-term effects of exercise

short-term effects

- breathing
- pulse rate
- circulation
- muscles
- sweating

long-term effects

- general well-being
- effects on the heart
- circulatory system
- breathing
- body composition
- muscles
- rate of recovery

Facts

There are a number of physiological changes that occur immediately following the onset of exercise. The OCR specification requires you to know about the areas specified below:

- breathing
- pulse rate
- circulation
- muscles
- sweating.

Key points

Breathing

- The rate of breathing rises quickly.
- In some cases this may begin before activity commences.
- More air is drawn into the lungs as the muscles involved in breathing work harder.
- The increased volume of air delivers more oxygen to the bloodstream and then to the working muscles.

Pulse rate

- The nervous system triggers a faster heart rate and a greater volume of blood is pumped around the body.
- The stroke volume remains constant but the heart beats faster.
- This greatly increases the volume of blood delivered to the muscles.

Circulation

- The circulation of blood increases as the level of activity rises.
- This is in response to increased demand for oxygen by the muscles.
- The major blood vessels dilate (become larger) to allow this to happen.
- Those blood vessels not involved in the activity will constrict (narrow).

Questions

1. Why do you think breathing and respiration rates sometimes rise before activity has begun?

2. Explain why the resting pulse rate of a fit person is likely to be lower than one who is unfit?

focus point

The pulse rate continues to rise until the oxygen being delivered to the muscles reaches the required level. In aerobic activity, the pulse rate then levels off if activity remains constant. In anaerobic activity, the event will be over before the pulse rate has risen to the level required by the (heavy) work rate. It will therefore continue to rise for some time afterwards. This is why continued (warm down) activity is advisable, as it helps to disperse blood from the muscle fibres and prevents pooling.

Muscles

- Blood vessels in active muscles dilate (become larger) to accommodate the increased bloodflow.
- Blood temperature rises and this produces more efficient muscle action.
- The graph here shows that a rise in blood temperature from 37°C to 41°C produces a 15 per cent increase in the performance of muscles:
    - this increases the blood supply to muscle tendons, reducing the likelihood of tears, strains or pulls
    - this process will have begun during the warm up.

Sweating

- Sweat production is accelerated during increased levels of physical activity.
- Sweat released via the sweat glands/skin pores helps remove impurities from the body.
- The evaporation of sweat at the skin surface contributes to body cooling.

Long-term effects of exercise

Facts

The more general long-term effects of exercise include:

- a fitter, healthier body
- an improved sense of well-being
- stronger bones
- more elastic tendons and muscles
- increased range of movement.

General well-being

- This refers to more general (e.g. not related to competition) benefits that improve our daily lives.
- We generally enjoy better health.
- We have better and more regular patterns of sleep.
- We have a healthier appetite.
- We have a generally more positive attitude to life and work.
- We are often less susceptible to everyday illnesses, aches and pains.

Effects on the heart

- These include the enlargement and strengthening of the heart chambers, a stronger heartbeat and a more efficient circulation.
- More specifically, long-term effects also include:
    - heart rate – a lower resting heart with a greater capacity for work
    - stroke volume – the stroke volume (the amount of blood pumped from the heart in one beat) can be double that of an untrained individual
    - cardiac output – larger stroke volume increases the blood processed per minute.

Did you know

That after a meal blood is diverted from the muscles to the digestive system.

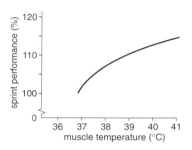

Performance in sprinting improves as muscle temperature increases

Did you know

That an active lifestyle when you are young will influence your health in later life.

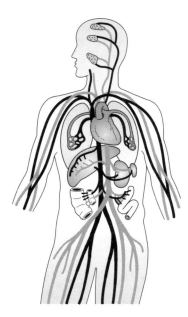

Improved respiration and circulation gets oxygen to the muscles far more efficiently

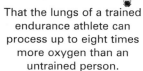

Did you know ❓

That the lungs of a trained endurance athlete can process up to eight times more oxygen than an untrained person.

Circulatory system

- Arteries become larger and more elastic.
- Blood pressure is reduced.
- More red blood cells produce more haemoglobin.
- There are lower levels of fat in the blood because the body has learned to utilise it as fuel.
- There is an increased capacity to process lactic acid during exercise.

Breathing

- There is an increase in the number of alveoli in the lungs.
- The lung capacity is therefore increased, allowing a greater volume of air (oxygen) to pass into the bloodstream.
- We are able to maintain higher levels of activity for a much longer period of time.
- There is an improvement in anaerobic capacity as there is more energy stored in the muscles.
- Gaseous exchange is considerably improved, so that carbon dioxide and other waste products are removed from the body more efficiently.
- We are less likely to become breathless when performing normal daily tasks.

Body composition

- Bones become stronger as a result of the increased levels of calcium production.
- Muscles and their tendons become stronger and far more elastic.
- If activity includes aerobic exercise, our body learns to utilise fat more efficiently as fuel energy instead of carbohydrate.
- Fat deposits are reduced, leading to a loss of bodyweight.

Muscles

- Muscles become larger (hypertrophy).
- This growth is governed by the nature of training and competitive activity.
- If heavy weights are lifted in training, muscle size will increase significantly.
- The using of lighter weights with more repetitions will increase muscular endurance.
- Fast-twitch muscle fibres also increase in size if training includes speed of movement.
- An increased network of blood vessels improves the supply of blood to the muscles; this is known as vascularisation or collateral circulation.
- Muscle cells store larger amounts of energy.
- Tendons and ligaments become stronger and more flexible.

Rate of recovery

- An accelerated recovery rate allows us to cope with more regular and increased physical demands.
- This capacity grows as new fitness levels allow even faster recovery (adaptability and progression).
- This leads to the faster repayment of oxygen debt and faster removal of lactic acid.

Questions

1. Why is an increase in blood supply and muscle temperature particularly significant in respect of muscle tendons?

2. How does the heart becoming larger and stronger result in an increased stroke volume?

3. How do the long-term effects of exercise improve the rate and efficiency of gaseous exchange?

Exam tips

You need to understand:

- how the body's systems respond to exercise in the short term, namely: breathing, pulse rate, circulation, muscles and sweating
- how the body's systems respond to exercise in the longer term, namely: general well-being, heart rate, stroke volume, cardiac output, circulatory system, breathing, body composition, muscles and rate of recovery
- how to monitor the above responses and display them in graphical or tabular format.

focus point

While all the above points are generally valid, some caution is necessary. Some individuals can become addicted to exercise and, as a result, can suffer from the pains, strains and other injuries associated with over-training. While it is clearly harmful to our health to take little or no exercise, it is also dangerous to go to the opposite extreme. Over-use injuries and tiredness can affect not only our ability to participate in sports and recreations but also our enjoyment of other everyday activities.

Key Words

physiological changes	stroke volume
constrict	dilate
cardiac output	haemoglobin
carbohydrate	lung capacity
blood vessels	hypertrophy
vascularisation	over-training

Potential hazards

Potential hazards

Facts

Humans encounter risk in many aspects of their lives and to attempt to remove risk entirely would be neither possible nor desirable. Absolute safety is rarely achievable. The challenge for education is that young people are properly prepared to manage reasonable risks with which they are faced and to help them develop the generic skills and awareness which may be usefully applied in any situation to enable their own and others' safety. (BAALPE, Safe Practice in Physical Education, 1999)

The OCR specification identifies a number of areas with which you should be familiar:

- court areas
- the gymnasium
- outdoor adventurous activities
- the playing field
- the sports hall
- the swimming pool.

 **points**

- Although your teachers are required to assess the risk potential in all the activities they teach, you also have a responsibility to be aware of any hazards that may be involved.
- The assessment of risk is a fundamental aspect of daily life.
- Even enjoyable activities are not exempt from unhappy outcomes.
- There are particular hazards associated with the environments in which activities occur.

Court areas

Facts

Hard court areas present the most common source of serious abrasions.

 **points**

- General litter, paper, drink cans and other sharp or broken objects can cause serious injury.
- On an 'open' site, these problems are not always caused by the school population.
- Other potential hazards may include:
  - broken/protruding strands of fencing
  - nails or other sharp projections

- buildings that are too close to court areas
- unstable portable posts or posts which encroach into the playing area
- surfaces affected by rain, snow, frost or inadequate maintenance
- projecting post-sockets which may be in the middle of another playing area
- unprotected adjacent windows or glazed walls.
- Get into the habit of 'sweeping' an area to ensure that any foreign objects are removed.

The gymnasium

Facts

- It is ironic that what is regarded as the most enjoyable indoor space in the school also has the potential to be one of the most hazardous.
- Many gymnasia were designed to be just that – gymnasia – not small sports halls!

 **points**

- Potential dangers can be greatly minimised by students accepting that they have a collective duty to behave responsibly.
- Fixed apparatus items often project into the working floor space, even when they are correctly stowed away.
- Inadequate storage space means that some portable apparatus/equipment cannot be stored easily.
- Footwear used for outdoor activities should not be worn in the gymnasium.
- Slippery, dusty or dirty floors are often the cause of accidents.
- Use by outside groups during the evenings and at weekends can add to the above problems.

focus point

The above are points on which it is reasonable to expect responsible students to co-operate with their teacher prior to, during and at the end of lessons. This will encourage a sensible attitude to a working environment that will benefit you not only in physical education but which hopefully will help prepare you for responsibility elsewhere in school and, later, in adult life.

Outdoor adventurous activities

Fact

The environments in which many of these activities take place are often harsh, remote, exposed and potentially dangerous.

 **points**

- There are a considerable number of possible activities under this heading, each of which may present its own potential hazards.
- Adventurous activities take place on land or on water (or possibly both).
- In either case, it is possible to establish certain general concerns:
  - the location may be remote

- it may be exposed to the weather and the terrain may well be difficult
- the way you behave, the way you are dressed and the way you communicate with others becomes far more important than in your normal everyday surroundings
- if you are a non-swimmer, you should ensure that your teachers and others in your group are aware of this
- if you suffer from agoraphobia, vertigo or conditions such as diabetes or epilepsy you should also find out whether it is advisable for you to take part in the activity.

Activities on land

- Land-based activities include:
    - assault courses and other 'challenge' activities
    - camping and/or expeditions
    - caving and potholing
    - cycling/mountain biking
    - horse riding/pony trekking
    - mountain walking and/or climbing
    - orienteering
    - rock climbing and abseiling
    - skating
    - skiing.

Activities on water

- If activities are taking place in or on water, considerations should include:
    - is the water enclosed (e.g. a swimming pool or a small boating lake)?
    - is the water open or coastal (how deep is it and are there dangerous currents)?
    - what are the safety procedures in the event of a capsize or other eventuality?
    - if the water activity is also in a remote area, the risk of exposure would also be relevant.
- Water-based activities include:
    - angling
    - canoeing and kayaking
    - rafting
    - rowing
    - dinghy sailing
    - windsurfing
    - sub-aqua
    - surfing
    - swimming
    - water skiing.

The playing field

focus point

Each of the activities above carries with it one or more potential hazards in addition to the general comments made at the start of this section. Any activity involving climbing, for example, will involve working at height and will carry with it fairly obvious hazards associated with that fact.

You should make yourself aware, as far as is possible, of any specific hazards associated with any activity you intend to undertake before embarking on it. No one else should be asked to be responsible for you if you are not prepared to be responsible for yourself.

Did you know

That a greater number of young people now take part in outdoor adventurous activities than ever before.

Fact

Playing field areas are the most difficult to close off effectively. It is therefore likely that risks deriving from outside use will be more common than elsewhere in the school.

 **points**

- Potential hazards include some of those referred to under Court areas.
- Animal faeces, broken glass, crushed drink cans and general litter are far more noticeable on tarmac and other hard areas than they are on grass playing fields, particularly on rugby pitches where grass is longer.
- It is important that students develop the habit of checking for hazardous objects prior to a lesson in order to ensure that any likely source of injury is identified and removed before activity commences.
- Other potential hazards include:
  - playing field areas that are close to buildings
  - long grass, bumpy or uneven surfaces and surfaces affected by frost, ice, snow or heavy rainfall
  - the use of temporary goal or boundary posts that are short enough to allow someone to fall onto them
  - portable goalposts (e.g. five-a-side soccer)
  - rugby posts without protective padding
  - corner flags that are not flexible and resistant to breaking
  - inappropriate equipment (e.g. indoor equipment)
  - smooth-soled footwear, particularly in contact sports.

Did you know

That local authorities became legally obliged to provide playing field space for schools following the 1944 Education Act.

The sports hall

> **Fact**
>
> A sports hall is effectively either a very large gymnasium or a very small sports field.

 **points**

- During activities involving projectiles, remember that greater velocity means added risk of injury.
- Students from other groups may be entering or leaving during activities.
- Use the viewing panels in doors to check that it is safe to enter before doing so.
- If it is normal for an activity to take place within a netted area, ensure that this is the case.
- As in a gymnasium, equipment that is not in use must be safely stored away.
- Surfaces with which performers are likely to come into contact should be free of projections.
- As in other areas, the co-operation of students is a crucial element of safe and sensible practice.
- If the complex includes other facilities (e.g. a fitness room), appropriate guidelines should be observed.
- The floor surface should be treated with the same care as that of a gymnasium.

The swimming pool

Facts

The hazards in a swimming pool are likely to come from two sources:

- the activity in the pool
- the pool and its surroundings.

 **points**

Pool-based activities

- The governing bodies of activities that take place in swimming pools (e.g. the ASA and the RLSS) publish clear guidelines on all aspects of safety and potential hazards.
- Irrespective of the activity in which you might be involved, the following points are extremely important:
  - do not enter the water until you are told and in the way that you are told
  - engage only in the activity that you are instructed to undertake
  - leave the water when and in the manner you are instructed
  - swimmers and canoes do not mix, other than for capsize/rescue drills
  - for personal survival activities, ensure that the less strong swimmers are closest to the poolside
  - in all pool-related activity, a sensible and responsible attitude is critical in reducing risk.

The pool and its immediate environment

- Your teacher or instructor has responsibility for a whole group of students and it is totally unreasonable to expect him or her to be 'responsible for the irresponsible'.
- In all swimming pool areas, health and safety regulations require that definitive dos and don'ts are clearly displayed in appropriate areas.
- As a general guide, these potential hazards might include:
  - wet floor surfaces around the pool and in showering and changing areas
  - general horse-play and any form of 'gymnastics', either in the water or on the poolside
  - diving boards and other poolside apparatus, particularly when other activity is taking place in the immediate area
  - the use of flippers, snorkels or masks (other than swimming goggles) by inexperienced swimmers
  - venturing out of your depth if you are a poor or novice swimmer
  - submerged grating or grilles.

Questions

1. What type of footwear should not be worn when taking part in an outdoor team game on grass? Explain why.

2. Why should flippers or snorkels not be used by inexperienced swimmers?

3. Why is it important that students co-operate in identifying potential hazards before an activity?

4. Why are outdoor adventurous activities potentially more hazardous than normal PE lessons?

5. Why is communication important in physical activites?

6. Give a reason why gymnasium equipment should be stored away when not in use.

7. What personal information should you provide before spending a week at an adventure centre?

Exam tips

You need to understand:

- how to identify potential hazards in physical activity and performance situations
- how to identify potential hazards in the following areas: court areas, the gymnasium, a range of land- and water-based outdoor adventurous activities, the playing field, the sports hall and the swimming pool
- the reasons why there are potential dangers in the above activity areas
- how to make others aware of the risks involved in physical activities.

Key Words

sweeping
fixed apparatus
portable apparatus /equipment
remote terrain
projectiles
netted area
capsize/ rescue drills
foreign objects
inappropriate equipment
exposed hazardous objects
complex personal survival activities

Prevention of injury

Minimising risk

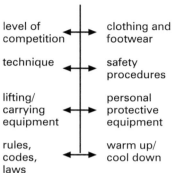

minimising risk

level of competition ←→ clothing and footwear

technique ←→ safety procedures

lifting/ carrying equipment ←→ personal protective equipment

rules, codes, laws ←→ warm up/ cool down

Facts

- There are risks associated with all physical activity, as well as with the environment in which it takes place.
- Whilst it is impossible to completely remove the risk of injury, we can ensure that this is minimised.
- There are factors that must be considered by teachers and coaches, but students also must contribute to safety by taking a responsible attitude to safe practices.

The OCR specification identifies a number of areas with which you should be familiar:

- appropriate level of competition
- correct clothing and footwear
- correct technique
- knowledge of appropriate safety procedures.

- lifting/carrying/placing equipment
- personal protective equipment
- rules, codes, laws
- warm up/cool down

 **Key points**

Appropriate level of competition

- There are obvious dangers associated with young people being placed in competitive situations that are not appropriate because of their age, sex or physical stature.
- Age:
  - Young people mature emotionally and intellectually at different rates.
  - Girls mature emotionally and intellectually much earlier than boys.
  - Many games and sports have intellectual and strategic components.
  - Although age-group competitions are the norm, this means of deciding what is appropriate competition can be unsatisfactory in some activities.
- Sex:
  - Traditionally, sports and recreations are single-sexed.
  - Mixed activities are now far more commonplace.
  - Many girls mature physically much earlier than boys.
  - When boys begin to mature physically, some mixed activities do constitute an unnecessary risk.
- Size:
  - Size can sometimes be used to advantage.
  - It is sometimes a disadvantage where mobility and speed are crucial.
  - Great differences in size are possible among students of the same age.
  - This is far more relevant in activities involving physical contact than it is in others.
  - Ironically, boxing is one of the few activities that classifies weight and age.

Did you know ?

That tag rugby was developed as a safe game for both sexes.

Correct clothing and footwear

- In most sports, clothing fulfils three purposes: it is an expression of group or team identity; it provides protection from the elements and/or during warm up; it is appropriate/safe for the activity for which it is intended.
- Clothing:
  - Team uniform helps create an identity within the team.
  - It is also an expression of pride in what the team represents (e.g. the school).
  - For normal lesson activities, clothing should be sensible, safe and affordable.
  - In some instances, clothing must satisfy certain religious/cultural requirements.
  - Any additional clothing should be removed once full activity is under way.
  - Additional protective clothing may be necessary (e.g. on redgras or Astroturf).
  - The wearing of fashion items – just to be 'cool' or different – is not acceptable.
- Footwear:
  - Footwear must be appropriate for the activity.
  - Unsuitable footwear can be dangerous.
  - Footwear should always be laced-up properly.
  - Tight-fitting footwear can cause blisters and long-term foot problems.
  - Spikes or studs should be securely fixed and rough edges made safe.
  - Outdoor footwear should not be worn for indoor activities.
  - Footwear should be cleaned regularly.
- Items of personal adornment:
  - These items should not be worn whilst taking part in physical activities.
  - Where they cannot reasonably be removed, they must be covered so that they cannot cause injury.
  - Long hair should be held securely in place by a means that will not cause discomfort to the wearer or others.
  - Where physical contact is either intentional or possible, fingernails should be clipped short.
  - Health and safety regulations apply to rings, earrings, etc. and other items of personal adornment in school activities just as they do in the adult workplace.

Correct technique

- Correct technique improves performance and reduces the risk of injury.
- Personal injury:
  - Poorly executed technique can result in serious injury to the performer.
  - In some activities (e.g. gymnastics), competency is acquired gradually.
- Injury to others:
  - A poorly directed discus can result in serious injury to anyone who might be in its way.
  - A badly hit hockey ball can have equally disastrous results.
  - Good technique not only aids good performance but it can also reduce the risk of injury to others.

Did you know ?

That in many sports the correct technique is also the safest.

Knowledge of appropriate safety procedures

- Safety procedures must be followed in order to minimise the risk of accident or injury.
- These procedures involve:
  - risk assessment – are the inherent risks controllable; are they reasonable or acceptable?
  - identification of potential hazards (see pages 68 to 73)
  - prevention of injury – can the likelihood of injury be reduced by attention to the points above or in the way that an activity is performed?
- Safety procedures are important in:
  - setting up/preparing for an activity – is the equipment safe and is it set up safely?
  - ensuring safe working practices – is the activity carried out within approved guidelines?
  - completion and clearing away – is equipment dismantled and stored correctly and safely?
- You should have developed a thorough knowledge of the safety procedures that apply to your own specialist activities and others in which you may be involved.

Questions

1. Give an example of a poorly executed sporting skill that might cause injury to someone.

2. What form of rugby is recommended for mixed participation?

3. Why is it unsafe to play team games in footwear that is not properly laced up?

4. Name two items of personal adornment that should not be worn during physical activity. Explain why.

5. Why are ordinary training shoes considered to be unsuitable for a day's walking expedition over rough, mountainous terrain?

Lifting/carrying/placing equipment

- Equipment is often most dangerous when it is being moved.
- Key points: co-operation and safety.
- It is impossible for some items of equipment or apparatus to be moved safely without the co-operation of others, and there are clear risks of serious injury if this is not done in a precise, safe manner.
- Lifting and carrying items of gymnasium apparatus, and fixing and securing heavy items such as movable wall bars and beams – these are just two tasks with which you should be familiar.
- Items such as javelins, discoi and shot pose other problems.
- In respect of any activity in which you are involved, you should know how to:
  - take out and move or carry equipment safely
  - make secure and use equipment safely
  - put away equipment safely.

Personal protective equipment

- It is irresponsible not to use the protective equipment that is both recommended and reasonably available.
- This topic raises three main issues:
  - the need to take reasonable measures to ensure sensible personal protection
  - consideration for the feelings of an opponent who may injure you simply because you fail to act responsibly by wearing protective equipment
  - whether, in some instances, the wearing of protective equipment encourages a less responsible attitude to the way you perform.

Rules, codes, laws

- The primary aims of the rules of any sport include:
  - the establishment of a framework of rules, which as far as possible ensures fair competition
  - setting clear guidelines as to what is safe and fair practice
  - identifying a range of sanctions to be used against offenders.
- Rules are a framework within which all should attempt to perform, for safety reasons.
- There is increasing pressure on élite performers to adopt a 'win-at-all-costs' attitude.
- This does not justify breaches of rules or codes of conduct which may cause serious injury.
- In all sports, but particularly those involving physical contact or heavy, dangerous implements, each individual has a responsibility to control their own behaviour.
- What is unsafe or unfair practice is outlined in the rules of each sport in which you take part.
- Sanctions are necessary in order to reinforce safe practices and deter/punish dangerous ones.

Warm up/cool down

- A warm up is not only important as a preparation for good performance but is also a crucial element in the avoidance of injury, particularly in the first few moments of activity.
- A poorly or hastily executed warm up routine can result in injury at the onset of full activity.
- Gradual and controlled cool down helps in achieving the most effective recovery from physical exertion.
- This helps to reduce the likelihood of stiffness and soreness and, thus, subsequent injury.
- These procedures are important for all participants, whether they are young people, élite performers or senior citizens.
- For athletes who sometimes train more than once a day, it is even more important that full and correct warm up and cool down procedures are part of their routine.
- Massage and other manipulatory procedures are often employed to assist in both preparation for and recovery after activity.

Good personal hygiene

Facts

Lack of attention to personal hygiene may not directly cause injuries, but it can certainly produce almost as much discomfort. Even minor infections can disrupt training and affect competitive performance.

 **Key points**

- Apart from the normal routine of personal grooming, a simple personal hygiene regime in connection with sporting and recreational activity can make all the difference.
- Shower, using soap, after all physical activity.
- Dry off thoroughly before dressing.
- Never wear the same clothes during and after physical activity.
- Ensure that all personal items of clothing are washed after each use.
- The most common infections that affect active people include athlete's foot and verrucae:
  - athlete's foot – a form of fungi that infects the area between the toes and the soles of the feet
  - verrucae – a form of wart which become embedded into the feet because of the pressure caused by walking
  - in both cases, infection can be greatly minimised by properly drying the feet after showering or bathing.

Questions

1. Give two reasons why it is irresponsible not to use personal protection equipment.
2. Give two reasons why rules are necessary in sporting activities.
3. Why is it inadvisable to dispense with a warm up before physical activity?
4. Identify one aspect of personal hygiene in connection with sporting activity and explain why you consider it to be important.

Key Words

age
sex
size
protection
personal
  adornment
risk
  assessment
approved
  guidelines
lifting/carrying
  /placing
  equipment
fair
  competition

appropriate
  competition
team identity
unsuitable
  footwear
correct
  technique
identification
  of potential
  hazards
personal
  protection
responsibility
warm up
cool down

Exam tips

You need to understand:

- how to reduce the risks involved in activities and thereby reduce the likelihood of injuries
- what footwear, clothing and personal protection equipment are appropriate for any activity you might undertake
- how to conform to the rules appropriate to the activity and how to carry, manage and operate equipment properly
- how to prepare yourself both physically and mentally for any activity in which you may take part
- the importance of good personal hygiene as an aid to preventing minor infections such as verrucae and athlete's foot.

Injury treatment

Signs and symptoms

Facts
• Signs are those things you can see.
• Symptoms are those things the injured person can tell you about.

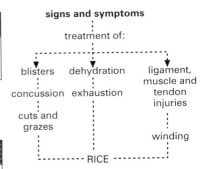

signs and symptoms

treatment of:

blisters   dehydration   ligament, muscle and tendon injuries

concussion   exhaustion

cuts and grazes

winding

RICE

Treatment of simple performance injuries

Facts
• You are not expected to treat injuries.
• The OCR specification requires you to recognise and explain the treatment of simple performance injuries only.

 **points**

Blisters
- These form when the skin repeatedly rubs against another surface.
- A tear occurs between the layers of the skin and fluid seeps into the space.
- The most common site for blisters is on the feet, but the hands can also be affected.
- If the skin remains unbroken, protective padding is the best immediate treatment.
- Larger blisters may need to be drained under medical supervision.
- If the skin is broken, the blister should be disinfected, covered and medical advice sought.

Concussion
- All knocks to the head should be regarded as potentially dangerous.
- Concussion is the result of a severe blow to the head, causing jarring of the brain against the skull.
- Signs:
  - The subject may be unconscious, although this is often short-lived.
  - He or she may appear to be drowsy or drunk, and may be confused.
  - He or she may have some difficulty in staying awake and speech may be slurred.
- Treatment:
  - All cases of suspected head injury must receive immediate medical attention.
  - This should be done via a member of staff or other person in charge of your group.
  - Try to help the subject retain consciousness, but refuse requests for drinks.
  - No other treatment should be administered other than to keep the injured person warm and comfortable.

Questions

1. What is the difference between the signs and symptoms presented by an injured person?

2. At what stage should a blister require medical attention?

3. What type of injury to the head requires immediate medical attention?

Cuts and grazes

- Cleansing and the application of an antiseptic dressing is enough to promote healing in minor cuts.
- With deep cuts there is also the risk that a muscle, tendon or major blood vessel may be severed.
- In the latter circumstances, the affected part should be immobilised and medical treatment sought immediately.
- The primary aim of those present would be to stem any blood flow until help arrives.
- If pressure applied at the site of the wound does not achieve this, a tourniquet should be applied at the nearest pressure point above the injury.

Dehydration

- Dehydration is most likely to result from the combination of excessive perspiration (fluid loss) and an inadequate fluid intake.
- Signs:
  - Excessive sweating.
  - Rapid heart rate.
  - Vomiting.
  - Sunken eyes.
- Symptoms:
  - Sickness.
  - Dizziness.
  - Feeling of extreme weakness.
  - Difficulty in maintaining balance and co-ordinating movement.
- Treatment:
  - Sensible and immediate fluid intake (rehydration).
  - Seek specialist medical diagnosis (immediately if there is no apparent recovery).
  - Loss of more than 15 per cent of body fluid which remains untreated can cause seizure, brain damage or in some cases death.

Exhaustion

- Exhaustion is often associated with extreme environments or events involving considerable endurance; the body has used up its available energy stores and fluids.
- Signs:
  - Extreme difficulty in co-ordinating movement.
  - Low temperature.
  - Dilated pupils.
  - Weak pulse.
  - Pale, moist skin.
  - Fainting spells.

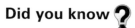

Did you know

That dehydration and exhaustion sometimes present very similar signs and symptoms.

The conditions for dehydration are often found in endurance events

- Symptoms:
  - Headaches.
  - Sickness and/or dizziness.
  - Extreme physical weakness.
- Treatment:
  - In cases involving extreme heat or cold, immediate steps should be taken to cool or warm the subject.
  - Whether or not the location is remote, medical advice should be sought immediately.
  - Where medical help is delayed, an appropriate (warm or cool) environment should be maintained.
  - This can be done by wrapping the person in blankets or additional clothing to maintain body warmth or by loosening clothing, fanning and applying cold/warm cloths to the forehead, armpits and groin.
  - Electrolyte drinks or slightly salted water can be sipped, if the person agrees.
  - No alcohol or caffeine should be given as these interfere with the body's temperature regulation.

Questions

1. A deep cut with considerable bleeding should be treated in which manner?

2. What is meant by the term 'rehydration'?

Injuries to ligaments, tendons and muscles

- A strain is an injury to a muscle or tendon caused by overuse, excessive force or over-stretching.
- Sprain:
  - An injury to a ligament often caused by a wrench or twist.
  - Sprains most commonly occur at the ankle, knee or wrist joints.
  - The most effective treatment is that based on RICE (see below).
- Tear:
  - A complete or partial rupture of a ligament, muscle or tendon fibres.
  - Treatment involves immediate immobilisation (RICE) followed by possible surgical repair.
- Note that all three injury types present similar signs and symptoms, hence similar initial treatment.

Winding

- This is usually caused by a blow to the abdominal area, paralysing the diaphragm.
- Signs include great difficulty in breathing, doubling over at the waist and inability to speak.
- The subject should be placed in a reclining, seated position until the ability to breathe is recovered.

RICE

- The RICE method is recommended as early treatment for all minor injuries and can help promote recovery almost from the onset of injury.

- Rest:
  - The first aim is to immobilise the injury and reduce/stop bleeding.
  - In the case of minor strains or muscle injury, rest should last at least 24 hours.
  - The application of strapping and other supports during rest is not the province of the first aider, who should render only such treatment as is necessary to stabilise the injury.
- Ice:
  - Do not apply ice directly to the skin as it may cause skin burns.
  - Ice cools the tissues, constricts the blood vessels and restricts bleeding in the affected area.
  - It may also help to reduce swelling in the case of muscle or joint injuries.
- Compression:
  - This is achieved by firmly binding the affected area, but not so tightly as to constrict circulation entirely.
  - If a tourniquet is used it should not be applied at the site of injury.
- Elevation:
  - Elevation is obtained by raising the injured part so that gravity assists in the drainage of tissue fluids.
  - This also reduces blood flow to the site of the injury.

RICE – rest, ice, compression and elevation (a/w to be supplied)

Questions

1. Explain what is meant by:

   a) a sprain
   b) a strain
   c) a tear

   in muscle or joint injuries.

2. Explain the principles behind the four elements of RICE treatment.

Exam tips

You need to understand:

- how to recognise and treat simple performance injuries
- how to recognise and differentiate between the signs and symptoms of common injuries such as cuts, grazes and blisters; and muscle, tendon and ligament injuries
- how to apply simple first-aid principles such as RICE to the above injuries
- how to recognise the signs and symptoms of dehydration, exhaustion and concussion, and the relevant simple first-aid procedures that might be appropriate in such situations.

Key Words

signs	symptoms
blisters	concussion
pressure point	dehydration
fluid intake	rehydration
exhaustion	electrolyte
immobilis-	winding
ation	diaphragm
RICE	stabilise
tissue fluids	

Notes on the OCR Physical Education exam paper

Introduction

At the end of your course you will take the final written paper, which is worth 40 per cent of your overall mark. There are different exam papers for each specification:

- Physical Education (1970)
- Physical Education: Games (1971)
- Physical Education: Games (Short Course) (1070).

You will sit the exam for which you have been specifically prepared and which, on completion, will be marked by an external marker. The marks you gain in the written exam will be added to your coursework marks to give an overall mark that will determine your final grade.

This section provides you with practical advice and guidance in preparing for the exam. It does this by outlining the structure of the question papers so that there are no hidden surprises when you sit the exam. It explains the type of questions in the various exam papers and gives you an example of the kind of question paper you can expect. Finally, it offers you guidance on how to revise and prepare yourself for the exam, with advice on dos and don'ts in the examination.

The papers for each of the three specifications differ slightly in that the Physical Education (1970) paper may make reference to physical activities and/or games, whereas the Physical Education: Games (1971) and Physical Education: Games (Short Course) (1070) papers will refer to games only.

The structure of the exam papers

The Physical Education (1970) and Physical Education: Games (1971) papers are both 1 hour 45 minutes long and consist of two sections, A and B. The Physical Education: Games (Short Course) (1070) paper is 1 hour long. It also has two sections, but there are fewer questions. The papers will be in booklet format, and each question will include a space underneath for your answer. The possible mark to be awarded is shown against each question. You will find specimen question papers for Physical Education (1970) and Physical Education: Games (Short Course) (1070) on pages 86 to 96. When you read through the questions you should also note the comments in the right-hand column – these offer guidance on answering the questions. They also explain any differences between the three papers.

Section A

Section A consists of both short-answer and structured questions on the three units of the Programme of Study. Marks will show an incline of difficulty – the first question carries one mark, for which a very short answer is required, whilst subsequent questions carry more marks and require more detailed answers.

In the Physical Education (1970) and Physical Education: Games (1971) papers there are 20 marks allocated for this section, whilst in the Physical Education: Games (Short Course) (1070) paper Section A is worth 14 marks.

Section B

Section B consists of three questions, each covering one of the three units of the theoretical Programme of Study. Each question is structured and shows an incline of difficulty. The marks for each of the three questions vary to reflect the subject content in the three units in each specification.

In the Physical Education (1970) and Physical Education: Games (1971) papers, the marks awarded for question B1 are likely to be about 23 as this is the largest unit of study. Question B2 is likely to carry approximately 18 marks and question B3 approximately 15 marks. In both specifications there are 56 marks for the questions in this section, plus a possible further 4 marks for the 'quality of written communication', making a total of 60. In the Physical Education: Games (Short Course) (1070) paper the questions in this section are likely to be worth 14, 10 and 8 marks respectively. This gives 32 marks, plus a possible further 4 marks for the 'quality of written communication', making a total of 36.

How much time should be spent on each question?

All questions are compulsory. Therefore, you can plan in considerable detail how much time you intend to spend on each section. You may wish to use the following as a guide when answering questions from either the Physical Education (1970) or the Physical Education: Games (1971) papers:

- Section A (normally about 10 questions) – allocate 20 to 25 minutes
- Section B1 (normally about 7 questions) – allocate 30 to 35 minutes

Section B2 (normally about 6 questions) – allocate 25 to 30 minutes

Section B3 (normally about 5 questions) – allocate 15 to 20 minutes.

As all questions carry marks, you *must* attempt to answer them all. However, you should spend longer preparing your answers to those questions with higher marks. If you spend the time as indicated above, this would leave between 5 and 15 minutes to check your answers and make final adjustments.

The Physical Education: Games (Short Course) (1070) paper is shorter, so it carries fewer questions. You may wish to use the following as a guide during the exam:

Section A (normally about 6 questions) – allocate 12 to 14 minutes

Section B1 (normally about 5 questions) – allocate 15 to 18 minutes

Section B2 (normally about 5 questions) – allocate 12 to 14 minutes

Section B3 (normally about 3 questions) – allocate 10 to 12 minutes.

This would leave between 2 and 10 minutes to read through your answers and make final adjustments.

What type of questions can you expect in the exam?

The questions in each of the papers have been written to test your knowledge and understanding of the principles of physical education and how you apply them to practical situations. You should be able to draw on the knowledge you have gained in the theory units you have been taught in the classroom and in practical lessons. None of the questions have been written to trick you.

Many of the questions will ask 'why' or 'how'. For example:

Why is muscle strength important in sprinting? (1 mark)
How can you improve leg strength for sprinting? (2 marks)

Other questions may call for an explanation or description. These are likely to carry more than one mark and it is important that you give a full explanation or description in your answer.

Remember that, irrespective of the question, the examiner only wants to know whether you know the answer. It is therefore important that you answer as accurately as possible in the space provided. Should you need extra space for your answer, you may use the additional pages at the end of the question paper, but remember to clearly indicate the question number.

Some questions may be based on an activity or game with which you may not be familiar. This should not affect your understanding of the question. You should be able to transfer your knowledge from other activities in order to answer the question. The following is an example of such a question:

John is a very enthusiastic hockey player who is keen to improve his overall performance level. Describe how social facilities can influence John's future progress in hockey. (4 marks)

Although the question refers to hockey, it could easily have been based on any of a number of activities. You should be able to answer the question using your knowledge of another activity or game. You will not be asked technical questions, such as how to demonstrate a skill in hockey.

Some questions may be of a data response type. These questions may be based on information presented in a graph, chart, picture or table. You will be expected to interpret the information and draw conclusions. Here is an example:

This table shows the results of four fitness tests performed by four Year 10 students.

	Standing long jump (cm)	Heave on the beam (max)	Sit-ups (in one minute)	50m sprint (secs)
John	180	8	28	7.8
Carl	210	10	28	7.3
Ajay	160	5	23	8.6
Luke	200	5	27	7.5

a) Which test measures arm and shoulder strength? (1 mark)

b) Which test measures abdominal muscle strength? (1 mark)

c) Which student scored the highest in the standing long jump and 50-metres sprint tests? (1 mark)

d) Which two of the above tests are good indicators of sprinting ability? Explain why. (4 marks)

You may have recorded test scores during your practical activities, but you may not have had the opportunity to compare them with those of others. It is therefore important that you familiarise yourself with different forms of data presentation.

It might be assumed that a high figure is the best score, but this is not always the case. For example, the fastest sprinters have lower sprinting times. Look at the information carefully and do not make any rash decisions before you have given careful consideration to the question. Try to become familiar with figures represented on bar charts and graphs, and how to place individuals in ranked order using different types of data. The specimen question papers on pages 86 to 96 may help you to understand this further. Alternatively, you should seek help from your teacher.

What is meant by the 'quality of written communication', and how is this assessed?

When you take any written exam you should realise that you are being tested not only on your subject knowledge but also on how well you express yourself in written English. It is therefore important that you always try to write good English, paying particular attention to your spelling, punctuation and grammar. This is referred to as the 'quality of written communication'.

In the exam papers two questions, B1 and B2, are set specifically to test the quality of your written communication. The examiner can award up to two extra marks for each of these questions based on the following assessment criteria:

- 1 mark for candidates who spell, punctuate and use the rules of grammar with reasonable accuracy, and use a limited range of specialist terms appropriately
- 2 marks for candidates who spell, punctuate and use the rules of grammar with considerable accuracy, and use a good range of specialist terms adeptly and with precision.

You should write your answers in a clear and logical manner. Try to use complete and accurate sentences and check your spelling carefully. Also, use extended prose where appropriate when answering higher mark questions. If the use of bullet points seems appropriate, use them but ensure that sentences are grammatically correct. When you have finished, remember to take some time to read through your answers to ensure that they are worth the extra marks available.

What will the exam paper look like?

You can expect the paper to look very similar to the following specimen papers. Only one significant change has been made to the specimen papers – the spaces normally provided for candidates' answers have been omitted. An indication of the number of lines for the answers has been given.

Make sure you read through the 'Instructions to candidates' section. These explain how to complete your personal details on the first and subsequent pages. You should also read through the 'Information for candidates' notes, which remind you of the marks awarded for different parts of the paper.

On the right-hand side of the following specimen papers an additional column of 'Guidance notes for candidates' has been added to offer you advice on completing the questions in the various sections.

Specimen exam papers and answers

Physical Education 1970 paper

General Certificate of Secondary Education

PHYSICAL EDUCATION 1970

Additional material: None
Candidates answer on the question paper

TIME   1 hour 45 minutes

Candidate name	Centre Number	Candidate Number

INSTRUCTIONS TO CANDIDATES

Write your name in the space above.
Write your Centre number and Candidate number in the boxes above.
Answer all the questions.
Write your answers in blue or black ink in the spaces provided on the question paper.
Read each question carefully and make sure you know what you have to do before starting your answer.

INFORMATION FOR CANDIDATES

The number of marks is given in brackets ( ) at the end of each question or part question.
The number of marks for this question paper is 80.
You will be assessed on the quality of written communication in **Section B, questions B1 and B2**.
Four marks will be available for the quality of written communication.

(*Note*: The cover of the Games (Short Course) (1070) paper differs only in the title and the time allowed [1 hour]).

Section A

Answer **all** questions in this section.

1   Identify **one** outdoor physical activity in which the following aspects of fitness would be particularly important.

   a)   Good cardiovascular fitness. *(1 line)* (1)
   b)   Good arm strength. *(1 line)* (1)

2   Explain **one** way in which drugs can reduce performance in a physical activity. *(3 lines)* (1)

3   Explain **one** way in which fitness and health can be affected by regular exercise. *(3 lines)* (1)

4   Explain how the deltoid muscle produces movement in a physical activity. *(3 lines)* (2)

5   Explain, using an example, how antagonistic muscles work to enable movement to take place during a normal physical activity. *(4 lines)* (2)

6   Identify **two** factors related to aerobic exercise. *(4 lines)* (2)

Guidance notes for candidates

● All the questions are compulsory, so try to answer each one.

● The number of lines provided for your answer is a good indication of how much space you need. However, if you need more space, use the extra pages at the end of the question paper.

● The number in brackets at the end of the line indicates how many marks are available for this question. Where the mark is 2 you should try to mention at least two different points in your answer, three points for 3 marks, etc.

● There are the same number of questions in the Physical Education: Games (1971) question paper as there are in the Physical Education (1970) paper, but only 6 questions in the Physical Education: Games (Short Course) (1070) paper.

7   Give **two** reasons why it is important to consider where pupils are standing when watching a demonstration of a practical skill. *(4 lines)* (2)

8   Explain any **two** of the FITT principles and how they can be applied to a training programme in order to improve performance. *(4 lines)* (2)

9   Explain the role of the national centres of excellence in supporting the development of sporting excellence. *(4 lines)* (2)

10 Explain the signs and symptoms of common muscle and tendon injuries and describe a simple treatment. *(8 lines)* (4)

(TOTAL 20)

Section B

Answer **all** questions in this section.

B1: Factors affecting participation and performance

Tom is a keen badminton player who represents his school and local club in competitions.

a) Describe the role that Tom's school might play in furthering his interest in badminton. *(2 lines)* (1)

b) Explain the beneficial effects that movement and exercise has on Tom's joints. *(4 lines)* (2)

c) Explain how the skills of a novice (beginner) can be distinguished from the skills of a top-level performer. *(4 lines)* (2)

d) Describe the positive and negative effects that tradition and culture can have on Tom's participation in sport. *(5 lines)* (3)

e) Explain how different types of feedback in practice situations can improve Tom's performance. *(8 lines)* (4)

- The questions have been framed within the context of badminton. This should not prevent you from answering the questions, even though you may not have a great deal of experience of playing the game.

- In all cases, the game chosen will be popular in school.

- This section carries 2 additional marks for the quality of written communication. You should therefore take greater care in structuring and writing your answers and checking your spelling, punctuation and grammar.

f) Explain the social reasons why there is increased leisure time. *(8 lines)* (4)

g) Explain how Tom's circulatory system responds to the physical demands of playing a game of badminton. *(12 lines)* (7)

(TOTAL 23)

B2: The relationship between health, fitness and physical activity

John has been a member of the local football team for more than 20 years, but at 42 years old he has decided to discontinue playing as he has become more prone to long-term injuries. Knowing the importance of exercise and fitness, he has decided to use running and swimming as his main forms of exercise. He has set himself manageable target times, with the aim of reducing them by 2–3 minutes over a six-week period. John always does a warm up and cool down after each session.

Week two of John's training programme is as follows:

	Mon	Tue	Wed	Thurs	Fri	Sat	Sun
Activity	5km run	1000m swim	5km run	1000m swim	5km run	1000m swim	Rest day
Target time	28 min	30 min	28 min	30 min	28 min	30 min	–

a) Which type of fitness is John mainly concentrating on in his training programme? *(1 line)* **(1)**

b) Name **one** principle of training that John uses in his training programme. *(2 lines)* **(1)**

c) i) Explain why you think that John is careful to warm up before each training session? *(3 lines)* **(1)**

   ii) Describe the kind of activities that John might do during a ten-minute warm up for one of his swimming sessions. *(4 lines)* **(2)**

d) In order to provide a little more variety to his training programme, John has decided to introduce interval training into one of his swimming sessions each week. Explain what interval training is and how it might be applied in a swimming session. *(4 lines)* **(2)**

e) Every three weeks John intends to use the 12-minute run to test his fitness. Describe how the test is carried out and how the results can be used to assess his own fitness level and compare his fitness with someone else who has also taken the same test. *(8 lines)* **(4)**

f) Describe the long-term training effects that John can expect his heart, circulatory and respiratory systems to benefit from if he continues with this training programme. *(12 lines)* **(7)**

(TOTAL 18)

- The questions are based on a description of John, a former footballer, and the training programme he has devised in order to keep himself fit and healthy.

- You should read the introduction carefully because clues to some of the questions may well be there.

- Many of the questions should relate to what you have done in your training. Use your experience as well as your knowledge to answer the questions as accurately and as fully as possible.

- Read through your answers to ensure that your spelling, punctuation and grammar are accurate in order to gain the extra marks.

B3: Risk assessment in physical activity

Whilst playing hockey for her school, Jennifer turned quickly to tackle an opponent, slipped and fell awkwardly on her left hand. Immediately she felt a sharp pain in her wrist that was later painful to touch. The referee immediately stopped the game and sent for medical assistance.

a) Describe the symptoms of Jennifer's injury. *(1 line)* **(1)**

b) Some accidents happen and clearly cannot be avoided. What measures could Jennifer take in future to lessen the risk of the same accident happening again? *(4 lines)* **(2)**

c) Describe the potential hazards that can occur when playing hockey on a synthetic (artificial) surface. *(6 lines)* **(3)**

d) If you were required to provide immediate first aid for Jennifer's injury, describe the form of treatment. *(8 lines)* **(4)**

- The introduction describes a typical injury in a sport – in this case, hockey.

- Read the introduction twice in order to understand the scene that is being set.

- Draw on your own knowledge and experience of accidents that may have happened to you or to others in sport, but only use them if they are relevant to the question.

e) Describe how hockey players minimise the risk of injuries to different parts of the body. What preventative measures do they take? *(10 lines)* **(5)**

(TOTAL 15)

Physical Education 1970 answers

In the following notes, in some cases more than one answer has been given to show the scope of possible responses that a candidate may give. The OCR mark scheme will cater for this and examiners will adopt a positive method of marking, i.e. credit will be given for what candidates know.

Section A

1 a) Cross-country running, middle/long distance athletics events, association football, hockey.
   b) Athletic throwing events, rugby, cricket.

2 ● Side effects on the heart and other vital organs that can have detrimental effects on how they function, thus affecting performance.
   ● Narcotic analgesics can mask pain, allowing athletes to train and damage muscles and other organs unknowingly.
   ● Diuretics can eliminate water from the body to a sometimes dangerously low level.

3 ● Improved functioning of all vital organs, especially the circulatory, respiratory and muscular systems. All body systems are beneficially affected to some degree.
   ● Exercise is likely to improve all fitness components.
   ● Exercise can have psychological benefits, including a feeling of well-being.
   ● Exercise can have other beneficial effects, including better sleep and improved appetite.

4 ● The deltoid muscle contracts to raise the upper arm above the head.
   ● The movement might be raising a weight above the head, or holding a javelin in the extended position prior to throwing.

5 Antagonistic muscles work together to enable movement, with one muscle contracting whilst the other is relaxing. An example of an antagonistic movement is the biceps and triceps muscles working to cause extension and/or flexion of the elbow joint. Physical activity might be press-ups. The biceps and triceps contract alternately to raise or lower the body. (The example of antagonistic muscles in the legs or other parts of the body could also be used.)

6 ● Aerobic exercise needs a constant supply of oxygen for it to take place.
   ● Exercising over a long period of time involves the aerobic energy system.

● Activities such as cross-country running, continuous games activity, distance swimming and cycling are aerobic activities – the competitor needs to breathe in oxygen for it to take place.
● During aerobic exercise the body is able to remove waste products (including lactic acid) at a rate which is at least equal to the rate at which they accumulate.
● Aerobic exercise improves cardiovascular fitness.

7 ● To visualise clearly the whole pattern of movement skill.
   ● To recognise the parts of a complex skill and the timing, e.g. a tennis serve that involves a correct stance, ball throw, racket movement and contact with the ball, and timing.

8 ● Frequency (F) – how often does the training take place?
   ● Pitched at a certain level of intensity (I) – how hard?
   ● Over a set period of time (T) – duration.
   ● To be of a certain type (T) – related to the performance to be improved.

9 ● Specialist training facilities and equipment in five locations.
   ● Each caters for different types of sports, e.g. the National Water Sports Centre caters largely for water-based sports.
   ● Mainly caters for élite performers, although some allow the public to use the facilities.

10 Common muscle and tendon injuries are strains, sprains, tears, cuts, abrasions, lacerations and contusions. Signs are swelling, discolouration, bleeding (in the case of cuts, etc.) Symptoms are pain at the point of injury, lack of mobility in the affected part of the body. Treatment:

   ● **RICE – R**est injured part; apply **I**ce to constrict blood flow and reduce pain and swelling; apply **C**ompression to prevent fluids draining to injured part; **E**levate the injured part to limit the blood flow to the injury and to promote drainage of other fluids.
   ● For cuts – application of a sterile dressing.

Section B1

a) ● Provide use of school facilities.
    ● Opportunities for further practice/coaching/competition.
    ● Local, regional and national courses/competition and provision.

- Goal setting/preparation to maintain motivation.
- Analysing and improving performance, including advice on diet, training/practice times.

b)
- Maintains flexibility in joints.
- Encourages the lubricating effect of synovial fluid in the joint.
- Ligaments, tendons and bones grow stronger to adapt to increased workload.

c) Novices tend to:
- be inconsistent and often perform movements slowly
- put a lot of effort into executing a skill, but produce less effective performance
- be unable to adapt the skill quickly when necessary.

Top-level performers can:
- perform skills with a high level of consistency, accuracy and efficiency
- perform skills with apparently little effort or energy expenditure
- adapt skills to meet other needs as required.

d) Positive effects of tradition and culture:
- Encouraging all sections of society (irrespective of race, religion and gender) to participate.
- Providing facilities, encouragement through teaching, publicity and the media.

Negative effects of tradition and culture:
- Females dissuaded or banned from participation.
- Restrictions on forms of dress, colour of skin (apartheid) and disability.

e) Intrinsic feedback – derived from acquired experiences. A feeling of whether the skill was performed correctly, detected through feedback from sensors in muscles and joints.

Extrinsic feedback – largely comes from teachers/coaches and video evidence in the form of what they see and hear.

Knowledge of performance – perception of performance derived from external sources.

Knowledge of results – perception of performance based upon outcomes/results.

f) Social reasons for increased leisure time include:
- workers now work fewer hours per week
- they get longer holidays each year

- more workers take early retirement
- the unemployed can use leisure facilities.

The drive for increased leisure time has come about as a result of:

- improved healthcare, enabling more people to participate, including the disabled
- an interest in personal appearance and body image, which encourages more people to participate
- a big increase in leisure facilities provided by both local and private organisations
- media and social pressure to take active part in leisure pursuits.

g)
- The heart beats faster in response to the demands for oxygen at the muscles.
- Blood is pumped to wherever needed, particularly muscles.
- Peripheral arterioles and venules constrict, diverting blood to working muscles.
- Restricted flow of blood to certain organs where there is less need during exercise.
- Blood returns to the heart via veins.
- Oxygenated blood is pumped to the muscles.
- Blood returning to the lungs is reoxygenated.

Section B2

a) Cardiovascular fitness.

b) Overload – John intends to reduce his target times over a six-week period.

c) i)
- His age may make him more susceptible to injury if he does not warm up thoroughly.
- John recognises the need for a warm up.

ii)
- Gentle freestanding exercises, arm and shoulder rotation, squats, trunk-twisting movements on the side of the pool or in the water.
- Gentle kicking exercises at the poolside for flexibility and technique.
- Short swims using different strokes to raise pulse rate.

d) A method of training involving repeated periods of exercise followed by rest/less intense exercise, e.g. a 100m swim, normally at 85–100 per cent effort, followed by a 2–3 minute rest, repeated 6–10 times.

e)
- A test carried out on a marked track, e.g. 400 metres.
- Markers are placed at intervals of 100 metres.
- Start watch as the run begins.

- The aim is to run as far as possible, counting the completed laps around the track.
- Approaching 12 minutes mark – note laps and extra 100 metres completed. Record total distance.
- Total distance run can be assessed against the 12-minute run tables to indicate your fitness level.
- Other runners can carry out the same test and compare distances.
- This is a comparison of different peoples' fitness levels.

f)
- Increased efficiency of the heart, heart muscle grows, improved circulation, lower resting heart rate, increased stroke volume, increased cardiac output.
- Better and improved circulation to the working muscles.
- Better circulation of blood within the working muscles as a result of collateral circulation.
- More red blood cells improves oxygen transport; more oxygen means more energy to the muscles.
- Improved gaseous exchange in the lungs.
- Increased vital capacity, which means more oxygen breathed in and more carbon dioxide breathed out.
- Increased oxygen debt tolerance enables exercise to continue with less risk of fatigue.
- Skeletal, cardiac and pulmonary muscles are able to work longer before becoming tired.

Section B3

a) Pain from the injury and painful to touch.

b)
- Practising turning on the surface being used.

- Practising different tackling techniques.
- Checking her footwear to ensure she has a good grip with the surface.
- Carrying out a risk assessment on the surface if the weather conditions are wet or icy.

c)
- Playing when the surface is wet, icy or slippery.
- Playing in footwear which gives a poor grip on artificial surfaces.
- Playing in footwear that is worn, incorrectly tied, inappropriate or dangerous.
- Being unaware of/unprepared for the ball travelling faster on some surfaces – someone may be hit by the ball.
- Contact with the surface can cause friction burns and grazes.

d)
- Remove her from the playing area.
- Tell her to support the injured wrist with her other arm.
- Sit her down and apply RICE treatment, e.g. rest, ice, compression and elevation.
- Arrange transport to hospital for an x-ray to check for possible fracture.

e)
- Using shin pads to protect the legs.
- Using gloves and arm guards to protect the hands and arms.
- Using a mouth guard to protect the teeth.
- Goalkeepers using helmets and face guard.
- Goalkeepers using body (chest) protection.
- Players warming up thoroughly.
- Understanding the rules to avoid making errors of judgement when playing.
- Knowing the correct techniques to avoid accidents with sticks, e.g. dangerous stick play.

Physical Education: Games (Short Course) 1070 paper

General Certificate of Secondary Education

PHYSICAL EDUCATION: GAMES (Short Course) 1070

Section A

Answer **all** questions in this section.

1 Identify **one** outdoor game in which the following aspects of fitness would be particularly important.

   a) Muscular endurance. *(1 line)* (1)
   b) Cardiovascular fitness. *(1 line)* (1)

2 Describe under what conditions the training principle of reversibility would apply to a games player. *(3 lines)* (1)

3 Describe **two** potential hazards you would find in indoor games facilities. *(3 lines)* (2)

4 Explain the advantages of both active and passive flexibility training to a games player. *(3 lines)* (2)

5 Using a simple information processing model, explain the importance of feedback in learning skills in a game. *(4 lines)* (3)

6 Describe the multistage fitness test and explain how it might be used to assess the fitness levels of a team of games players. *(4 lines)* (4)

   (TOTAL 14)

> **Guidance notes for candidates**
>
> - All the questions are compulsory, so try to answer each one.
>
> - The number of lines provided for your answer is a good indication of how much space you need. However, if you need more space, use the extra pages at the end of the question paper.
>
> - The number in brackets at the end of the line indicates how many marks are available for this question. Where the mark is 2 you should try to mention at least two different points in your answer, three points for 3 marks, etc.
>
> - Your answers must relate to a game or game situation.

Section B

Answer **all** questions in this section.

B1: Factors affecting participation and performance

Gemma is a novice tennis player who has recently joined a local tennis club in order to receive additional tennis coaching.

a) Describe the characteristics of a novice tennis player. *(2 lines)* (1)

b) Explain how the tennis coach might help Gemma to improve her skills in practice situations. *(4 lines)* (2)

c) Explain the importance of two basic abilities in promoting more advanced skills in tennis. *(4 lines)* (2)

d) Describe the processes that Gemma has so far gone through in learning the skills of tennis and the processes that she will need to go through in order to perfect her skills. *(5 lines)* (4)

e) Explain how Gemma's coach might use extrinsic motivating factors to improve her performance in tennis. *(10 lines)* (5)

   (TOTAL 14)

> - The questions have been framed within the context of tennis. This should not prevent you from answering the questions, even though you may not have a great deal of experience of playing the game.
>
> - In all cases, the game chosen will be popular in school.
>
> - This section carries 2 additional marks for the quality of written communication. You should therefore take greater care in structuring and writing your answers and checking your spelling, punctuation and grammar.

B2: The relationship between health, fitness and physical activity

The following graph shows the heart rate of Sam, a member of Bankside High School's Under-16 Rugby team, during a typical training session. Some parts of the training session have been identified.

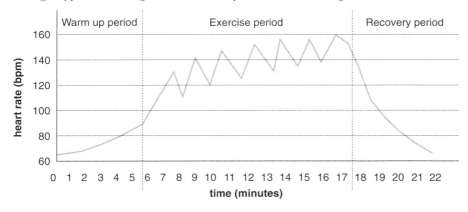

a) Why is it necessary to warm up thoroughly before taking part in vigorous exercise? *(2 lines)* (1)

b) Explain how you would take your partner's pulse rate during the recovery period of a training session. *(2 lines)* (1)

c) What is Sam's pulse rate:
  i) at the end of the warm up period? *(1 line)* (1)
  ii) at the highest point during the exercise period? *(1 line)* (1)

d) Sam's heart rate during the exercise period would seem to suggest a certain type of training. Explain what this type of training is and the immediate effect that the training is having on the heart during the exercise period. *(6 lines)* (2)

e) Explain how different tests might be used to evaluate Sam's overall fitness and his suitability to play in certain playing positions in rugby. *(10 lines)* (4)

(TOTAL 10)

- The questions are based on a description of Sam, a team member, and the results of his heart rate monitored during a rugby training session.

- You should read the introduction carefully because clues to some of the questions may well be there.

- Many of the questions should relate to what you have done in your training. Use your experience as well as your knowledge to answer the questions as accurately and as fully as possible.

- Read through your answers to ensure that your spelling, punctuation and grammar are accurate in order to gain the extra marks.

B3: Risk assessment in physical activity

Mrs Evans, the nurse at Bentley Hills High School, has been asked to record the number of accidents to pupils playing games during one school year. She has decided to show the likely causes of these accidents. Her findings are shown on the bar chart below.

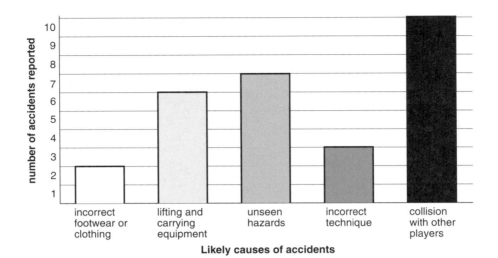

Serious accidents occurring during games lessons, 1999–2000

a) How many accidents in games lessons did Mrs Evans record during the year? *(1 line)* (1)

b) Which cause of accidents had the fewer incidents? *(2 lines)* (1)

c) Explain what precautions you would take to lessen the risk of future accidents happening to you if you are required to lift and carry equipment for a games lesson. *(6 lines)* (2)

d) Using examples from **two** different games, explain the different ways in which players might use personal protective equipment to lessen the risk of injuries occurring to particular parts of the body. *(8 lines)* (4)

(TOTAL 8)

- The introduction describes the kind of survey that might be carried out to discover the main causes of accidents in school over a period of time.

- Read the introduction twice in order to understand the scene that is being set.

- Draw on your own knowledge and experience of accidents that may have happened to you or to others in sport, but only use them if they are relevant to the question.

Physical Education: Games (Short Course) 1070 answers

In the following notes, in some cases more than one answer has been given to show the scope of possible responses that a candidate may give. The OCR mark scheme will cater for this and examiners will adopt a positive method of marking, i.e. credit will be given for what candidates know.

Section A

1 a) Rugby union, rugby league, water polo.
   b) Association football, hockey, netball.

2 ● Player unable to train, resulting in a decline in fitness.
   ● Illness or injury.

3 ● Sports hall – equipment left lying about; floors may be slippery due to water or too much floor wax.
   ● Gymnasium – protruding fixed equipment such as nets, wall bars, etc.; other equipment that has to be negotiated during lessons, e.g. boxes, benches, mats, etc.
   ● Swimming pool – slippery floors in all parts of the pool area; shallow areas of the pool that present dangers for divers.
   ● All areas – hazards that arise due to pupils being inappropriately dressed.

4 Advantages of active flexibility training:

   ● You recognise the need for flexibility training.
   ● You know how much mobility certain joints need and perform exercises for that purpose.

   Advantages of passive flexibility training:

   ● Can exert more pressure on the ligaments and tendons of joints to achieve the range of flexibility required.
   ● All parts of the body can be totally relaxed whilst the passive flexibility exercises are taking place, thus allowing greater freedom of movement.

5 ● Feedback is the information received after a movement has taken place. (Draw the input, decision, output, feedback diagram to explain the role of feedback.)
   ● Feedback can provide internal and external feedback.
   ● Feedback can provide knowledge of results (the success or failure of a movement).
   ● Feedback can provide knowledge of performance. This essential internal feedback can come from internal receptors such as balance centres in the head and muscle spindles.
   ● Feedback can be audible (guidance possibly from the teacher).

● For feedback to be useful it needs to be as instantaneous as possible, not confusing, and restricted to one or two simple straightforward points.

6 ● The test (often referred to as the bleep test) is a measurement of cardiovascular endurance (aerobic capacity).
   ● The test is carried out by running up and down a measured 20-metre course.
   ● The participants try to keep pace with an electronic bleep at the end of each 20 metres.
   ● Every two minutes or so there is a pause and the time interval is shortened between the bleeps, so the runner has to work harder to keep pace with the bleeps.
   ● Participants drop out when they cannot keep pace with the bleep at a certain level. They record the level they have achieved.
   ● The maximum level possible is 21, achievable by only the very fittest.
   ● This test might be used to measure the fitness levels of different players, e.g. forwards or backs, by seeing which levels they are able to achieve. A coach/teacher might then decide that those with a high level of fitness are more able to play in a certain position, e.g. open side flanker, where cardiovascular endurance is very important.

Section B1

a) ● Inconsistency.
    ● Inability to adapt skills.
    ● Skills often performed slowly.
    ● Timing is erratic or slow.

b) ● Identify the skills that Gemma is having difficulty performing.
    ● Break complicated skills down into small parts and practice the parts. Later put the parts together as a whole.
    ● Get Gemma to practise the skills slowly and then gradually increase the speed.
    ● Video Gemma's performance and point out her weaknesses in order to improve them.

c) Choose two from speed, agility, co-ordination, flexibility, balance and reaction time.

    ● Speed – need to be able to move about the court to both attack and defend shots from opponent.
    ● Agility – ability to turn quickly to return a shot and counter attack or attack the net.
    ● Co-ordination – the ability to perform complicated movements such as the serve, the backhand return, sliced volley, etc.

d) Gemma has gone through the processes of learning by:

- part, part-whole and whole learning
- looking at demonstrations and then copying the movements
- trial and error.

To improve further, she will need to:

- seek guidance from a coach/teacher
- practise
- review her own performance and improve any weaknesses.

e) The coach may offer the following extrinsic means:

- incentives such as certificates, prizes, rewards
- competitions and/or tournaments
- playing for money or trophies
- other incentives such as foreign travel
- the opportunity to play against more able players.

Section B2

a) Warm up:

- Prepares the body both physically and mentally for more strenuous exercise.
- Raises the temperature of joints and muscles.
- Makes joints more flexible, muscles more supple and less likely to tear.
- Allows the blood to flow more freely around the body and reach the working muscles.

b) Place index and second finger over the radial artery at the wrist. Press the radial artery and count the number of beats in one minute. This is the pulse rate. The carotid artery may also be used. Press the same two fingers against the carotid artery where it runs down the sterna mastoid muscle. Count the number of beats per minute.

c) i) 90 beats per minute.
   ii) 160 beats per minute.

d) Type of training:

- Shown by a period of exercise of about one minute where the pulse rate rises followed by a similar period of less intense exercise when the pulse rate drops. This is repeated seven times.
- This is anaerobic in nature.
- Characteristic of interval training.
- Period of intense exercise followed by a period of recovery, repeated seven times.

e) Overall fitness test may include both health-related and skill-related fitness components:

- Cardiovascular endurance – multistage fitness test or 12-minute run.

- Speed – timed 60m sprint.
- Strength – measure how much a person can lift, press or squeeze in a single effort.
- Muscular endurance – maximum heaves on a beam or sit-ups.
- Flexibility – measure the range of movement at a particular joint.
- Agility – timed run around a set out obstacle course.
- Balance – timed measurement of equilibrium (e.g. stork stand test).
- Co-ordination – performing a hand-eye or foot-eye skill test (e.g. juggling).
- Speed of reaction – the ruler-drop test; the sprint start.

Different tests may be more applicable to certain positions:

- Flankers could be tested using the cardiovascular fitness test.
- Scrum halves – the agility test.
- Centres and wings – the sprinting test.
- Props and hookers – the muscular endurance test.

Section B3

a) 28 accidents.

b) Incorrect footwear or clothing.

c) Lifting and carrying equipment:

- Only lift and carry equipment if told to do so and under the supervision of the teacher.
- If lifting equipment such as boxes, work as a team and lift together.
- Never run with equipment that is heavy or awkward to move.
- Never lift heavy equipment with a round back.
- Use your legs as the main muscular lifting force and keep your back straight.

d) Personal protective equipment in different games may include, for example:

- football/hockey – the use of shin pads to protect the legs.
- rugby – shoulder pads or padded jerseys to protect the shoulders and collar bones in tackles; gum shields to prevent injuries to teeth and mouth.
- cricket and hockey goalkeepers – helmets to protect head (and face) from injuries from contact with the ball; gloves to protect the hands; body padding (upper thigh, chest and forearm) to protect different parts of the body.